"Poppa" Psychology

"POPPA" PSYCHOLOGY

The Role of Fathers in Children's Mental Well-Being

Vicky Phares

Westport, Connecticut
London

Library of Congress Cataloging-in-Publication Data

Phares, Vicky.
    "Poppa" psychology : the role of fathers in children's mental well-
being / Vicky Phares.
        p.   cm.
    Includes bibliographical references and index.
    ISBN 0-275-96367-5 (alk. paper)
    1. Father and child.   2. Child psychology.   3. Fathers—
Psychology.   I. Title.
BF723.F35P48   1999
155.9′24—dc21   98-33614

British Library Cataloguing in Publication Data is available.

Library of Congress Catalog Card Number: 98-33614
ISBN: 0-275-96367-5

First published in 1999

Praeger Publishers, 88 Post Road West, Westport, CT 06881
An imprint of Greenwood Publishing Group, Inc.

Printed in the United States of America

The paper used in this book complies with the
Permanent Paper Standard issued by the National
Information Standards Organization (Z39.48–1984).

10 9 8 7 6 5 4 3 2 1

To my parents

CONTENTS

PREFACE

———————————————•———————————————

I became intrigued with the study of fathers (or more correctly, the lack of study of fathers) when I was an undergraduate at the University of California, Los Angeles. Since that time, a wealth of information has been established through intensive research projects and clinical investigations. Yet there is still much that we do not understand about fathers. This book is an attempt to summarize what we do know and to help call for more investigation into what we don't know. It will, I hope, inform readers on a personal level as well as on an intellectual level.

Personally and professionally I have been lucky enough to have been surrounded by people who have served as great role models. My parents, Bill and Rita Phares, provided a strong and stable family from which we all could grow. My siblings, Bill, Julie, Rita, and my siblings-in-law, Mary and D.J., have all helped me to see the many ways in which families can flourish over the years. My nieces and nephews, Holly, Timothy, Jeremy, Nakieta, Talisa, and Abby (!), have confirmed for me that the next generation will be even better than preceding generations. My graduate students have taught me more about dedication and commitment (as well as the current fashion trends) than I ever hope to teach them. My mentors and friends from graduate school and the academic life have shown me that success can be measured both by the quality of your work and by how much you enjoy hanging out with your partner and playing with your kids and the dog.

And speaking of a dog, some kids, and a partner, I am proud beyond belief to be part of the new and improved Owen-Phares family. Snickers is a role model in her perseverance. She has shown time and time again that if you hold the tennis ball in your mouth and look lovingly at a human for long enough, someone will inevitably play ball with you. On the human side, Nikki and Kelly are the most wonderful, well-adjusted, caring, creative, athletically skilled, and amusing teenagers I have ever known. I am honored to be their stepmother. My husband, Chuck, is more than I ever hoped for. In addition to being an incredible dad to Nikki and Kelly, he is a warm, supportive, nurturing, and tolerant husband. Who else would put up with the wacky hours of writing and watching films? Of course, I guess I have to be just as tolerant when the new jazz CD project rolls around. We're a darn good team, eh?

INTRODUCTION

———————————————— • ————————————————

First of all, this is not a book about blaming fathers. One of the reasons for exploring problematic father-child relationships is to counterbalance the awful pattern of blaming mothers that exists in our professional and personal lives. Turning around and blaming fathers might feel comforting momentarily for some people, but it would prevent the possibility of an objective exploration of problematic father-child relationships.

Second of all, this is not a book about looking into the past and finding fault so that all of our present-day problems can be explained away. Too often these days, it appears that people are looking to place responsibility for their problems everywhere except in their own lives and in their own choices. This is not to say that early events in our lives don't influence our current functioning—they do. This is also not to say that survivors of childhood abuse should in some way be blamed for the abuse—they shouldn't. It is to say, however, that events in the past cannot be changed. Instead, what we do with those events, how we think about those events, and how we use those events to make us stronger in our present day lives is what is important. Apparently in reaction to the plethora of talk shows and the lack of personal responsibility many people take in their own lives, the Eagles' Don Henley and Glen Frey summed up the process nicely by suggesting that we all "get over it."

Third of all, this is not a book solely about childhood abuse and trauma. On a number of occasions I have talked to a new acquaintance about my work with fathers, and the first thing she or he asks is about sexual abuse. It appears that for many people, an overwhelming image of "fatherhood" is that of a father sexually abusing his child. Although sexual abuse is extremely important to understand in order to prevent such abuse and treat its victims, there are many aspects of "fatherhood" that are not abusive but that are important to explore.

Finally, this is not a book about trying to create two-parent families in every household in the United States. As a result of the men's movement and the pockets of conservatism in the country, a number of authors have called for a return to "traditional" families with an employed father and a full-time homemaking mother. This scenario may work for some families, but with less than 7% of families today fitting the "traditional" structure (with an employed father and a full-time homemaking mother), to call for a return to this "traditional" mold appears unrealistic and misguided. In addition, as Stephanie Coontz argues in her book entitled *The Way We Never Were: American Families and the Nostalgia Trap*, that type of happy nuclear family may not have been as happy nor as common as many people would like to believe. Currently, given that most fathers and mothers are employed out of necessity rather than out of choice, and given that many employed fathers and employed mothers would not give up their paid employment even if they had a choice, it seems counterproductive to wish for a family structure that has outlived its usefulness for so many families.[1]

Now that you know what this book is not, let me explain what the book attempts to be. Through reading this book, you should gain a better understanding of how fathers influence their children's lives in both positive and negative ways. In addition, the ways in which children influence their father's life will be explored. These interconnections between fathers and their children will be discussed for fathers who are present in their children's lives and for fathers who are no longer physically present in their children's lives. As in all family issues, the interplay between mothers and fathers will be taken into account when discussing children's mental health.

Because this is a book about fathers' and children's mental health, an important topic to cover is therapeutic help for mental health problems. Suggestions for effective therapy will be discussed for families when the children are still young as well as for adults who are dealing with childhood issues regarding their father. Finally, suggestions will be provided for how to help fathers and children (as well as mothers) in families of the future.

1

FATHERS IN PRESENT-DAY FAMILIES

The very words "my father" always make me smile.
—ANGELA CARTER

The only people who get blamed more than mothers for psychological problems and distress are mothers-in-law. We live in a culture where women, and mothers in particular, are held responsible for problems that develop in children's lives. This responsibility does not appear to stop when children reach adulthood. Turn on any daytime talk show and chances are that mothers will be blamed for at least some of the problems being discussed.

Fathers, in contrast, rarely receive a second thought and almost never receive blame for their children's problems. Even when fathers or father figures sexually abuse their children, mothers are often blamed for their failure to protect their children. The one problem area that has received a lot of attention for fathers and much less attention for mothers is the area of problem drinking. It is important to note, however, that there are meaningful associations between fathers' and children's mental health problems across a variety of areas. This book reviews the connections between mental health problems in fathers and children with a focus on understanding these problems rather than looking for someone to blame. Most mental health problems result from a variety of factors, so there is no simple answer to understanding the familial roots of problems in mental health. After trying to achieve an understanding of the father's role in the development of psychological problems, we will explore how problems can be prevented from occurring in the first place. Because the topic of fatherhood, or more specifically the absence of fathers, is so controversial these days, a brief discussion of fathers' involvement with their children is warranted.

WHERE HAVE ALL THE FATHERS GONE?

In popular books such as *Fatherless America: Confronting Our Most Urgent Social Problem* and *Life without Father: Compelling New Evidence that Fatherhood and Marriage Are Indispensable for the Good of Children and Society* and in many news reports in magazine articles, in newspapers, and on television, we learn that fathers in the United States are almost nonexistent in their children's lives. Although this is true for many children, the overwhelming majority of children have some contact with their father. Many people are surprised to learn that well over half of the children under 18 years of age in the United States live with both of their biological or adoptive parents. In addition, most children who do not live with their biological father have at least monthly contact with him. Although these numbers are lower than what many people consider optimal, a closer look at the trends in family constellations might help us gain a better understanding of families in America.[1]

When combining across all children in the United States who are under 18 years old, 61.1% of children live with both of their biological or adoptive parents, 10.8% live within a stepfamily, 24.2% live in a single-parent household headed by their mother, and 3.9% live in a single-parent household headed by their father. Family constellations, however, vary across ethnic and racial groups. For example, 56.3% of African American children live in a single-parent household headed by their mother, 29.3% of Latino and Latina children live with their single mother, and only 18.8% of Caucasian American children live with their single mother.[2]

For those children who do not live with both of their biological or adoptive parents, different patterns of visitation arise depending on whom you ask. For example, in a series of nationwide studies, Dr. Judith Seltzer and her colleagues found that noncustodial fathers consistently report more visitation with their children than the custodial mothers report about the noncustodial father. If you ask mothers, 46.7% report that their child's father visits with their child at least once a month. When the noncustodial fathers are asked, 56.4% report that they visit with their children at least once a month. Regardless of whom you ask, most children under 18 years old in the United States either live with or have contact with their biological or adoptive father. These demographic data suggest that although absent fathers are apparent in many communities and many families, they are by no means the norm for today's children in the United States.[3]

WHEN CHILDREN LIVE WITH BOTH PARENTS: SPENDING TIME AND TAKING RESPONSIBILITY FOR CHILDREN

No one should be surprised to learn that mothers continue to spend more time with their children and to have more responsibility for their children than do fathers, even in two-parent families. Many commonly held beliefs about fathers are born out in large-scale research studies, namely, that fathers spend less time with their children than do mothers, that fathers take less responsibility for the day-to-day care of their children than do mothers, and that fathers spend more time with their sons than with their daughters. There are, however, some commonly held beliefs about fathers that are not supported by research studies: that fathers spend more time with their teenage children than with their infants . . . they don't, and that fathers' lower time involvement means less influence on their children . . . it doesn't.[4]

First, let's explore fathers' time involvement with their children. Remember that this information is based on studies of groups of families, and many fathers spend either a lot more or a lot less time with their children than these studies would suggest. There are a number of ways to measure fathers' time involvement with their children. Time in direct interaction (e.g., time playing or talking with the child) is one way to measure time involvement. Time accessible to the child (e.g., time together in the house but watching television in separate rooms and not interacting directly) is another way to consider fathers' time with their children. Time spent in taking responsibility for the child (e.g., making doctor's appointments and making sure that the child gets to these appointments) is another way of measuring time involvement and responsibility.[5]

Across each type of measurement of time spent with children and of responsibility for children, mothers continue to spend more time with their children, to use their time with their children more for caretaking activities than for play, and to have greater responsibility for their children than do fathers. Although there are families who have worked out more equitable arrangements, the common pattern in families in the United States is that mothers spend significantly more time with their children than do fathers, whether or not the mother is employed outside of the home. Please note that the term "employment" or "job" is used to denote parents' nonfamily-oriented activities for which they are paid. Too often, women who are full-time homemakers are referred to as women who do not "work." As anyone with child care experience and household maintenance experience knows, taking care of children and a household can be more time consuming and energy consuming than any job for which people are paid. In fact, a number of writers have suggested that the term "working mother" is redundant.[6]

In two-parent families in which both parents are employed full time (and mothers' time involvement is set at 100% for the purposes of comparison), fathers spend about 33% as much time as mothers in direct interactions with their children and about 65% as much time being available and accessible to their children. When it comes to taking responsibility for the children's activities and well-being (e.g., making medical and dental appointments), fathers carry only about 10% of the responsibility that mothers carry. These patterns are even more exaggerated in families in which the mother is not employed.

How parents interact with their children also varies according to whether they are a father or a mother. Beginning in their children's infancy and continuing through their adulthood, mothers tend to serve more of a caretaking and comfort-giving role with their offspring, whereas fathers tend to be more of a playmate. Even when fathers are conducting caretaking activities, such as feeding the infant or dressing the infant, they are more playful in their interactions than are mothers. Interestingly, these different roles for mothers and fathers are more pronounced when both the mother and the father are present than when either is with the child alone. Specifically, when fathers are alone with their children and when they have primary responsibility for their children, their behavior is much more similar to mothers' behavior in terms of being responsible for caretaking activities and emotional support of the child. Studies of fathers who are the primary parent (either because they have chosen a nontraditional family arrangement where the mother is employed full-time and they are the full-time homemaker or because they received custody of the children after a divorce) suggest that fathers who are the primary parent partake in behaviors that are very similar to most mothers' behavior. These comparisons suggest that it might be the role that a parent takes on, either as a primary parent or as a secondary parent, that is more influential in guiding their behavior than whether the parent is a mother or a father.[7]

Contrary to popular opinion, most fathers spend more time with their infant children and decrease the amount of time they spend with their children as the child grows older. The same pattern is true for most mothers. Given the high level of time involvement required for care of an infant, by necessity fathers and mothers spend much more time in taking care of infants. As children grow older and can take on more responsibility for their own daily care, the direct caretaking time for fathers and mothers is decreased. Also, as children grow older, they tend to want to spend more time away from home with friends or in organized activities (such as sports, clubs, or church activities and later at a job or with a girlfriend or boyfriend). These developmental trends seem to be related to the greater intensity of the parenting role for fathers and mothers when their children are infants as opposed to when their children are toddlers, school-aged, teenagers, and adults.[8]

Fathers' involvement with their children differs according to whether the child is a boy or a girl. Popular beliefs that most fathers spend more time with their sons rather than their daughters are correct. Across all age groups, fathers show more interest in their sons' activities, they are more likely to be involved in leisure activities with their sons, and they spend more time talking with their sons than they do with their daughters. These patterns may in fact be related to fathers' personal and emotional investment in the family, given that parents with at least one son are less likely to divorce than parents without a son.[9]

These patterns of fathers' and mothers' involvement have been relatively stable for a number of years and seem to be similar regardless of ethnicity, regional location, or religious affiliation. For example, studies of African American families have found patterns of fathers' and mothers' involvement similar to those seen in studies of Caucasian American families. These patterns have also been shown in other Western cultures as well as in non-Western cultures.[10]

With fathers' involvement with their children lower than mothers' involvement, you might assume that fathers have much less influence in the lives of their children. This assumption is incorrect. There is relatively consistent evidence that the *quality* of interactions with children is much more important to the child's well-being than the *quantity* of interactions with children. This pattern is true for fathers' as well as mothers' time involvement with their children. In general, parents who are responsive to their child's needs, who encourage the child to interact with other people, who support the child's independence in an age-appropriate manner, who are warm, and who pay attention to the child while they are interacting with him or her tend to have children who are well adjusted. For both fathers and mothers, the quality of interactions is much more important than the quantity of interactions when considering the child's mental health.[11]

These findings may be reassuring to fathers and mothers who are employed and not able to spend as much time with their children as they might like. Given that most parents are employed out of necessity rather than out of choice, it seems pointless to torture parents (especially mothers, who usually get the brunt of this discussion) with the implication that they are "choosing" between employment and child-rearing activities. As mentioned earlier, the old idea of a traditional family constellation, with a father employed full time and a mother a full-time homemaker, is evident in less than 7% of families in the United States. Thus, professionals and nonprofessionals alike should stop comparing current-day families with a family constellation that is extremely rare given the economic and social realities within the United States today. In addition, even if mothers and fathers had more of a choice as to whether or not to be employed, the majority would apparently still seek some type of employment rather than choosing to be a full-time homemaker. The realities of families in current society suggest that more effort should be put into making sure that there are affordable, high-quality day care options for children rather than spending so much effort in wishing that things were different.[12]

WHEN CHILDREN DO NOT LIVE WITH BOTH PARENTS: SPENDING TIME AND TAKING RESPONSIBILITY FOR CHILDREN

Although the majority of children in the United States live with both of their biological or adoptive parents, there are 38.9% of children under the age of 18 who do not live with both of their biological or adoptive parents. This percentage further breaks down into 10.8% of children who live within a stepfamily, 24.2% who live with their single, separated, or divorced mother, and 3.9% who live with their single, separated, or divorced father. For children who do not live with their biological father, the father is often referred to as "absent." It is important, however, to consider that there are different forms of absence (e.g., physical absence, emotional absence, and lack of financial support) that may or may not be experienced by children who do not live with their biological father.[13]

Most of the interest in this area has focused on visitation patterns between noncustodial fathers and their children. Based on a national survey of over 1,500 families in which the parents had separated or divorced, noncustodial fathers from a dissolved first-time marriage reported that they had a fair amount of contact with their children. A total of 15.6% of the fathers reported that they had contact with their children several times a week, 16.8% reported seeing their children once a week, 24.0% said that they saw their children from one to three times a month, 18.4% said that they saw their children several times a year, 7.7% reported that they saw their children once a year, and 17.4% said that they no longer had any contact with their children. As might be expected, these percentages are a bit higher than the percentages reported by the mothers of these children. Mothers reported that 11.2% of the noncustodial fathers had contact with their children several times a week, 12.8% saw their children once a week, 22.7% saw their children one to three times a month, 21.7% saw their children several times a year, 12.9% had contact with their children once a year, and 18.7% no longer had contact with their children. Even though fathers reported somewhat higher contact with their children than did the mothers, fathers' reports and mothers' reports did not differ significantly when compared statistically. Overall, this study suggests that although fathers and mothers do not always see visitation eye-to-eye, a large percentage of fathers do continue to have some contact with their children after the dissolution of a marriage.[14]

As is the case with the survey just discussed, most surveys of visitation with noncustodial fathers include families from a variety of racial and ethnic backgrounds. Because of the larger percentage of African American children living with a single, separated, or divorced mother, there has been some specific attention to contact with fathers and father figures in African American families. One survey found that 21.5% of African American children had a biological father who had always been present in their lives, 22.8% had a father who was sometimes physically present and sometimes physically absent from their lives, and 55.7% had a father who had always been absent from their lives. The comparable figures for children who were not African American were 70.3%, 8.6%, and 21.1%, respectively. A majority of children who did not have a father present in their lives did have some type of father-figure in their lives, such as a grandfather, an uncle, or their mother's boyfriend. A total of 59.3% of African American children who did not have a father in their lives did have some type of consistent father figure in their lives. The comparable percentage for children who were not African American was 61.9%. This type of survey suggests that it is important to acknowledge many types of fathers in children's lives and to recognize that children who do not live with their biological father may still have a wealth of father figures in their lives.[15]

In his powerful book entitled *Streetwise: Race, Class, and Change in an Urban Community*, Dr. Elijah Anderson discussed the differences between the traditional "old head" in a community and the more contemporary "old head" in a community. Traditionally, an old head was an older man with a stable work life and family life who could impart appropriate values and wisdom to those in the community who needed guidance. More recently, because of unemployment, racism, and impoverished communities, a newer old head seems to be taking over. These new old heads seem to gain status through less than honorable activities, and they seem to impart less than ideal values. Anderson makes the case that the traditional old head used to serve as a father figure to many children and young people who did not have a father in their life. Unfortunately, the new old heads may be serving in this same type of role, but they may be imparting a value system that is not consistent with the best interests of the community or the individuals themselves.[16]

For children from all races and ethnicities, having contact with their father seems to be related to a number of factors both in the past and in the present. Children and adolescents were more likely to have greater amounts of contact with their father when the parents' marriage was lengthy, when fathers lived relatively close to their children, when the father-child relationship was low in conflict, when the father-mother relationship was low in conflict, when fathers were satisfied with their parental role, and when fathers felt that they had some influence over their children's lives. When problems in visitation do arise, both fathers and mothers believe that these problems are easier to deal with when father-child visitation is frequent and when the father has a history of consistent payment of child support. Interestingly, based on both fathers' and mothers' reports, children whose mother had not yet remarried seemed to have more contact with their noncustodial biological father than those children who already had a stepfather in their life. It may be that because of family dynamics and feelings of loyalty or jealousy, children have difficulty maintaining close relationships with more than two parental figures at any one time.[17]

Counter to what might be expected, fathers who were highly involved with their children before the divorce seem to follow a pattern of becoming more disengaged from their children after the divorce than do fathers who had been relatively uninvolved with their children during the marriage. Many fathers who were very emotionally involved with their children and who spent a lot of time with them before divorce seem to have grief reactions (e.g., feelings of depression and hopelessness) about the possibility of losing contact with their children after divorce. To protect themselves psychologically, many fathers seem to disengage from their children emotionally and seem to spend even less effort at trying to maintain a relationship with their children after divorce. It seems that these fathers feel that it is inevitable that they will lose contact with their children, and therefore they initiate the loss themselves rather than wait for the loss to happen gradually. Sadly, many of these fathers would not have to lose contact with their children if they were able to remain committed to staying involved. It is also important to consider that the children may be the ones who really lose when a highly involved father becomes a lot less involved after divorce. Children may perceive their father's disengagement as a direct rejection of them and they may experience grief reactions of their own. In these cases, it is important for fathers, mothers, and children to consider seeking professional help that could help them negotiate a visitation schedule that works in the best interests of all the family members.[18]

An interesting side issue in the topic of visitation is how the amount of time is evaluated. Therapists in training are taught to try to take the client's perspective rather than labeling the experience for the client. For example, if an adult client states that he or she has had five sexual partners in his or her life, the therapist should not jump in and say, "Wow, that many?" Nor should the therapist say, "Oh, too bad there have been so few." Rather, the therapist should let the client provide his or her own evaluation of the experience. The same interpretative issues have been raised in surveys of father-child visitation. The same pattern of visitation between fathers and children (weekly dinners and every-other-week weekend visits) has been described as "relatively limited" contact, "frequent" contact, and "very frequent" contact by various researchers. It would be interesting to see how children, fathers, and mothers evaluate these visitation patterns in comparison to how professionals label these visitation patterns.[19]

Like contact between fathers and children in families where the parents are still together, it is important to recognize that the quality of contact between fathers and their children is much more important than the quantity of contact between fathers and their children after parents are no longer together. There is also reason to believe that when a high degree of animosity exists between divorced spouses, visitation between fathers and their children can serve to overcome the adverse effects of this interparental animosity. In particular, if divorced parents were arguing a lot, but if the father had a great deal of contact with the child and did not put the child in the middle of the conflict with the mother, then children were better off psychologically than if there was a high degree of conflict and a low level of father-child visitation.[20]

Regardless of visitation schedules or even the absence of father-child contact, it is imperative that parents not put their children in the middle of their disagreements with each other. Nearly all parents, whether they are still together or not, will have disagreements that need to be addressed with each other. It is very harmful for the psychological well-being of children when parents put children in the middle of their conflict or when they fight a lot in front of their children. Parents should aim for trying to deal with highly emotional arguments away from their children. When conflict is present between parents, it is important that the child be able to learn constructive ways to resolve conflict rather than simply to be exposed to the conflict. As in so many other areas, children learn from watching their parents. If parents yell and scream and then storm out of the house to get away from the arguing, is it all that surprising that children learn to yell and scream and then try to escape (e.g., run away or slam the door as they retreat into their bedroom) when they are faced with a difficult situation? Children learn from what their parents do more so than what their parents say. The old adage of "Do as I say not as I do" is ineffective as a parenting strategy. Overall, parents can best help their children learn how to handle conflict by resolving it in healthy ways for themselves, especially when the conflict is between the two parents.[21]

One major area of potential conflict between parents who no longer live together is the payment of child support by the noncustodial parent, usually the father. Given that fathers and mothers often differ in their reports of father-child visitation, it is not surprising to find that noncustodial fathers and residential mothers also differ significantly in their reports of child support payments. In one national survey, a total of 85.8% of the noncustodial fathers reported that they had paid some type of child support within the past year, but only 63.8% of the mothers reported having received child support payment from these fathers in the past year. Based on a comprehensive survey by the U.S. Bureau of the Census, only slightly more than half of mothers with sole physical custody of their children were paid the full amount of child support awarded to them. Given that these payments are court ordered and are to be used for the child's basic necessities, these low rates of compliance with child support payments are abysmal.[22]

Unfortunately, it is most often the children who lose when noncustodial parents do not pay the appropriate amount of child support. As will be discussed in the next section, research on "father absence" has found that the significant problems shown by children after parental divorce are often due to the decline in socioeconomic status of children and their single mothers after divorce. Counter to what some noncustodial fathers might say, most noncustodial fathers make financial gains after divorce, whereas most children and custodial mothers make significant financial losses after parental divorce. One study found that during the first year after divorce, mothers and children experienced a 73% decrease in their standard of living, whereas fathers experienced a 42% increase in their standard of living. These financial losses often mean that children and their mothers have to move to substandard housing, which means not only disruption in children's schooling and friendship networks but also that children may have to attend poorer quality schools in more impoverished and dangerous neighborhoods. This pattern varies from family to family, but the important point is that nonpayment of child support can have direct negative effects on the well-being of the child.[23]

When noncustodial fathers' payments of child support are studied, interesting patterns emerge for fathers who do and do not pay the full amount of child support. Higher rates of payment of child support are associated with voluntary arrangements of child support (i.e., an arrangement established by both parents rather than by court order), joint custody legal arrangements, fathers who make over $50,000 per year, fathers who see their children relatively frequently, fathers who live in the same geographical area as their children, and fathers who do not have a poor relationship with their ex-spouse after the divorce. Fathers who were consistent in their payment of mandated child support were also more consistent with providing other types of financial and emotional support to their children, such as maintaining health insurance for the child, buying the child presents, and attending the child's sports and school events.[24]

In general, it is important for parents to try to keep the best interests of their children in mind when dealing with financial and visitation decisions after the parents separate or divorce. It takes much personal strength and inner resolve for disgruntled parents to put aside their differences in order to do what is best for their children, but it is imperative that they do so. No one in his or her right mind ever said parenting would be easy, and parenting is especially challenging when parents have a lot of negative feelings toward each other. Whenever possible, however, it is important to realize that even if parents are no longer married to each other, they continue to be co-parents to their children for the rest of their lives.

WHEN CHILDREN DO NOT LIVE WITH BOTH PARENTS: THIS ISN'T BEAVER CLEAVER'S FAMILY ANYMORE

These days there is a great diversity in family constellations, many of which have very little resemblance to what is considered the traditional nuclear family. One family constellation similar to the traditional nuclear family is a stepfamily. Approximately 10.8% of children in the United States live within a stepfamily, which usually consists of their biological mother and their stepfather. The circumstances around the creation of a stepfamily can differ greatly from family to family, but there is almost always some time for adjustment to the new roles created in these families.

In a survey of stepfathers, the majority (52%) said that it was as easy to love their stepchildren as it was to love their own children. Stepfathers were more likely to have fatherlike feelings toward their stepchildren if they had been in a parental role with their stepchildren from early in the children's lives, if they had their own biological children as well as their stepchildren living with them, and if they had a solid and happy relationship with their wife or partner (i.e., their stepchildren's mother). Stepfathers who felt more fatherlike toward their stepchildren had a more positive relationship with their stepchildren than did stepfathers who did not feel comfortable with their role as a stepfather.[25]

When the mental health of children in stepfamilies is considered, there are more similarities than differences across a variety of family constellations. Most of the work done in this area suggests that it is not the family constellation that influences children's mental health; rather, it is the lack of conflict and the strong support within families that helps children's better adjustment—regardless of the type of family in which they live. For example, when comparisons were made of young teenagers who lived with both of their biological parents, their biological mother only, or their biological mother and their stepfather, few differences were found in the teenagers' psychological health, goal directedness, and school functioning. If there was a great deal of interparental conflict or lack of emotional support for the teenagers, then the teenagers were more likely to have adjustment problems regardless of their family's constellation. Similar results have been found in a wide diversity of families from different ethnic, racial, and socioeconomic backgrounds. Given that so many families do not have an option of being a traditional nuclear family, it is encouraging to find that children can be well adjusted in a wide diversity of family arrangements.[26]

Similar patterns are seen in families headed by a single, separated, or divorced father. Approximately 3.9% of U.S. children under the age of 18 live with their single, separated, or divorced father. Whereas it used to be the norm, and often the law, that mothers were given physical custody of children after divorce, most states have moved toward gender-neutral laws in awarding custody. In the majority of cases, mothers still get physical custody or joint custody is awarded with primary physical responsibility being held by the mother. It is estimated, however, that by the year 2000 close to 1 million fathers will be raising their children by themselves.[27]

In a survey of over 1,000 single fathers, the majority of fathers (72%) said they felt comfortable with their role as primary caregiver, but 28% reported that they either felt uncomfortable or had mixed feelings about being the primary parent for their children. Unfortunately, because single mothers were not included in the study, a comparison of single mothers' feelings cannot be made. Single fathers tended to feel more comfortable with their role if they had more years in the role of primary parent and if they were satisfied with their own social life. Single fathers tended to feel less comfortable with their parenting role when they felt that their relationship with their child was deteriorating.[28]

A great deal of interest has been shown in the gender of the children being raised by single fathers. The primary question is whether there is any difference for boys or girls being raised by a single father. Research results are mixed in this area, with early studies suggesting that boys did better being raised by their single father and girls did better being raised by their single mother. More recent research has suggested that single fathers may be doing better with raising their daughters, but only if there are no sons in the household. When all these studies are combined, the overriding results seem to suggest that there is no easy answer to this question. Rather, it appears that regardless of family constellation, children are the most adjusted if they are being raised by a parent or parents who show an authoritative parenting style (i.e., showing warmth and affection while providing age-appropriate structure that is explained in a rationale manner). These same conclusions keep surfacing whether we are looking at family structure or determining the type of caregivers (e.g., single mothers, single fathers, married parents, grandparents, etc.) most beneficial for children.[29]

Another family situation that has received attention is when teenagers themselves have children. It is estimated that at least 10% of teenage girls become pregnant each year, and 60% of these girls choose to carry the pregnancy to term and either give the infant up for adoption or try to raise the infant themselves. The fathers of these children are mostly under 20 years of age themselves, but a trend in many communities now shows that girls are being impregnated by men in their 20s and 30s. States differ somewhat in definitions of child sexual abuse, but many of these adult men who are sexually involved with teenagers could be prosecuted for sexual battery of a minor. Many of the teens impregnated by older men know that their lover might get in trouble if he were reported, and therefore many pregnant teens choose to keep the identity of the father a secret. Unfortunately, this pattern has negative ramifications for the teen mother's ability to collect child support payments and may limit the father's legal rights if he is not listed on the birth certificate.[30]

With regard to whether teens impregnated by another teenager choose to keep the baby or give the baby up for adoption, teen fathers and the mothers of the pregnant teens seem to have a great deal of influence. Mothers of pregnant teenagers seem to have the most influence on the initial plan to keep or to give up the baby, but teen fathers seem to have more influence on whether the teen mother follows through on the initial plan.[31]

Boys who become fathers during their teen years differ from boys who do not impregnate anyone during their teen years. Teen fathers were more likely to have parents who were not interested in their education, to have had school difficulties in elementary and junior high school, to have been evaluated negatively by their teachers, and to have shown little interest in their own education. It is important to note that these educational difficulties occurred long before the pregnancy, which suggests that boys who are having difficulty at school might be targeted for early efforts in order to prevent teen fatherhood.[32]

When teen fathers' involvements with their children are explored, different patterns emerge depending on marital status and ethnicity. It appears that Caucasian American pregnant teenage girls are more likely to marry or live with the father than are pregnant teenage girls who are African American, Latina, or Native American. For those teens who do not marry or live with the father, contact with the child differs between ethnic groups. Caucasian American teen fathers were found to have significantly less contact and less involvement with their child than were teen fathers from other ethnic backgrounds when they did not live with the child. For all ethnic groups, greater involvement with the child was also associated with the child being younger, the father being younger, and the father being employed. Interestingly, whether the teen mother lived with her own parents did not seem to influence the teen father's involvement with his child.[33]

Most of the work in this area has relied upon teen mothers' reports of teen fathers' involvement with their child. One series of excellent studies that asked teen fathers about their own experiences was conducted with African American teen fathers. Based on their own reports, African American teen fathers who had higher self-esteem were more willing to take personal and financial responsibility for their child and seemed more psychologically prepared to serve in the parenting role. In addition, teen fathers who felt good about their own family of origin were more likely to take responsibility for their own offspring. African American teen fathers who were employed showed more nurturing and caring interactions with their children than did teen fathers who were not employed.[34]

Psychologists and other mental health professionals have called for greater parenting support for teen fathers and mothers. A number of programs have been tried around the country, but public funding is often discontinued even when the program has been shown to be successful. For example, these programs often teach teen fathers parenting skills, try to help teen fathers get and keep a job so that they can provide financial support for their children, help fathers to become more respectful of women, and help fathers become more responsible about their own sexuality. These prevention programs help not only the teen fathers but also the teen mothers and the children of teen parents by providing more stability in parenting and less likelihood of physical abuse of the children. In one survey of teen fathers, 95% of the boys said they would be interested in attending classes on how to be a father. Unfortunately, funding for prevention programs is often cut when financial constraints arise. Many professionals note that it is ironic that we should expect teen fathers (and mothers) to be responsible and good parents to their children and yet we provide little to no support for allowing these good parenting behaviors to occur.[35]

Another type of family arrangement that is gaining more attention these days is when children have a father who is gay or a mother who is lesbian. It is estimated that there are between 6 and 14 million gay fathers and lesbian mothers in the United States, but these numbers may be an underestimate because of parents' fears of losing their children were they to reveal their sexual orientation. Most often children are born into an ostensibly heterosexual marriage that eventually breaks apart because one of the parents realizes or acknowledges his or her sexual orientation. There are, however, a growing number of homosexual adults who are finding alternative ways of serving in a parental role, including artificial insemination and adoption. A great deal of research has gone into evaluating the children of gay fathers and lesbian mothers, and results of these studies are relatively clear cut. When compared with children of heterosexual parents, children of homosexual parents do not show any differences in psychological health, relationships with other children, or sexual orientation. The lack of differences in part results from similarities in parenting styles regardless of parents' sexual orientation. When comparing gay fathers and straight fathers, no differences were found in parenting styles or attitudes toward fathering. Yet, again, it appears that the quality of parenting is related more to child well-being than to personal characteristics of the parent—in this case, the sexual orientation of the parent.[36]

FATHER "ABSENCE" AND CHILDREN'S MENTAL HEALTH

Until about 20 years ago, a great deal of attention was paid to the differences between children whose father was "absent" from their lives (meaning that the children did not live with their father) and children whose father was "present" in their lives (meaning that the children lived with their father). There are two primary reasons why this line of research has been considered misguided. First, the findings that children in "father absent" homes were more psychologically disturbed than children in "father present" homes could be accounted for by a number of factors other than the absence or presence of the father (e.g., children's and single mothers' economic decline after divorce and the greater likelihood of interparental conflict in families that had experienced parental separation or divorce). As noted earlier, mothers and children usually suffer a significant decrease in standard of living after parental divorce, whereas fathers often enjoy a significant increase in standard of living after divorce. The decrease in standard of living that children experience after parental separation seems to be related to the greater problems many children face after parental divorce. In addition, consistent evidence shows that overt and unresolved conflict between parents is harmful to the mental health of children. Since most children in the "father absent" families had probably experienced interparental conflict whereas many of the children in the "father present" families had not experienced high levels of interparental conflict, the findings that children from "father absent" homes were more distressed than children from "father present" homes may have been based on the interparental conflict that they had experienced rather than on the mere "presence" or "absence" of the father.[37]

The second reason that "father absent" research has been discouraged in recent years is that parental absence and presence is not really an all or none characteristic. It doesn't take a Ph.D. in psychology to know that some fathers who do not live with their children are very physically, financially, and emotionally "present" in their children's lives whereas some fathers who live with their children are very "absent" from their children in a physical and emotional sense. There is some evidence to suggest that psychological absence from children is more related to children's mental health problems than is physical absence. For these reasons, greater attention has been paid to parental relationships with children regardless of the specific living arrangements of the family.[38]

Highlighting these problems in the "father absence" literature is not meant to deny the very real emotional pain many children and adults experience as a result of their father's emotional or physical absence. In his excellent autobiography entitled *Monster*, former Los Angeles gang member Sanyika Shakur (aka Monster Kody Scott) provided a heart-wrenching account of what it was like to grow up without a father in his life. Children and adults often struggle for many years to try to deal with an absent father, just as absent fathers must often struggle with the meaning of their absence. Suffice it to say that the physical and emotional presence of parental figures is a terribly important and emotionally volatile issue for many individuals in many different family constellations. It is important not to dismiss the real pain that children, fathers, and mothers experience as a result of parental separation and divorce or to staying in a family situation that is less than ideal.[39]

SUMMARY

Throughout the discussion of different family constellations, certain themes have arisen. The most significant theme is that the quality of parenting is more important than the quantity of parenting or the personal characteristics of the caregiver who is providing the parenting. Another theme that is consistent throughout much of the work with children and families is the importance of dealing with conflict in a constructive manner that does not place the child in the middle of feuding parents. In some ways, these themes can give us hope, given that many families cannot meet the standards of a traditional nuclear family and that healthy functioning is within the reach of families regardless of their living situation. In some ways, however, these themes can be seen as difficult because they suggest that parents must work hard at maintaining good relationships with their children, regardless of their marital situation. Based on a wealth of research findings, it appears that being raised by two biological parents who fight a lot is worse psychologically for a child than being raised in a single-parent household where there are low levels of conflict. Obviously, families need to consider what is in the best interest of themselves and their children before using research results to make any personal decisions such as divorcing or staying in an unhappy marriage. These themes do suggest, though, that raising well-adjusted children is within the grasp of any parent who is willing to work hard at his or her parenting and to seek help when needed.

2

WHEN THINGS GO RIGHT: FATHERS AND NORMAL CHILDHOOD DEVELOPMENT

— • —

*When I was a boy of fourteen, my father was so
ignorant I could hardly stand to have the old man around.
But when I got to be twenty-one, I was astonished at
how much he had learned in seven years.*

—MARK TWAIN

By definition, most children develop normally. What I mean is that professionals define normal behavior in children by looking at what the majority of children do at that particular age. Abnormal behavior, then, is defined as behavior that is unusual (and harmful or distressing) for a child of that age and gender and cultural background. To provide an example of the difference between normal and abnormal behavior, consider the following vignette:

Imagine that you are a therapist and you receive a call from a father who sounds frantic and is asking about therapy for his daughter. The father says, "I'm really worried about my daughter. She used to be really sweet and mild mannered, and now she goes into temper tantrums at the drop of a hat where she lies on the floor and kicks and screams until she gets her way. At other times, she seems to believe really strange things, like that her mother can make the sun rise in the middle of the night and that our puppy can read her mind. I'm worried that we've let her watch too many scary movies, because sometimes she'll wake up

in the middle of the night screaming her lungs out. We really
need help."

If you were the therapist, what would your first question be to this
concerned father? (Before reading further, you might want to take a
minute to jot down some questions you would want to ask the father.)
When I've done this type of exercise in psychology classes and when
I've observed the exercise in other professors' classes, students often
come up with questions like "Have there been any recent traumatic
events in the child's life?" "Are the parents married or divorced?" "Is
there conflict between the parents?" "Is there a history of psychiatric
problems in the family?" "Just what type of movies do you let your
daughter watch?" Usually, at least a few students will also ask jokingly
whether or not the family has insurance to cover the therapy.
     What most students also ask, and what you have probably already
identified as a crucial question, is, "How old is the child?" Those of us
who have raised our own children or who have worked with children
would already have recognized that most of the behavior described in
the vignette is considered developmentally normal for a very young
child (e.g., temper tantrums, magical thinking, and night terrors are
relatively common in young children), but would be considered quite
worrisome for a teenager (none of these three behaviors are common
for psychologically healthy teenagers). In fact, most developmental
psychologists and clinical child psychologists would probably argue
that "How old is the child?" is the most crucial question you can ask in
order to ascertain the normality or abnormality of a child's behavior.
     If you are worried about your own child's behavior, I would encour-
age you to seek out a mental health professional who can help determine whether or not your child's behaviors are outside of the range of
normal behaviors for a child of that age, gender, and family background. In order to get started, you might want to read the section in
Chapter 6 that is entitled "How to Find Help." Just because you contact
a mental health professional does not mean that your child or family
will automatically be involved in therapy. Most mental health professionals first try to determine whether or not therapy is necessary and,
if so, which family members should be involved in therapy. In addition to seeking professional help, one way of trying to determine if
your child's behavior is similar to that of age-mates is to ask the parents of children that are the same age as your child. Teachers also have
a wealth of information and experience in knowing about developmentally appropriate and inappropriate behaviors. If you are dis-

tressed about your child's behavior, I encourage you to seek out lots of resources for yourself and your child.

Now we will switch back to children and families without problems. In this chapter, father-child relationships will be explored for behaviors in children that are considered "normal." For each area of interest, notice that there is a wide spectrum of what is considered "normal" in children. Researchers on fatherhood have usually explored normative development by focusing on the age of the child—for example, fathers and their infants, fathers and their young children, fathers and their teenagers, or fathers and their adult children. This chapter, therefore, will follow these categorizations. Note that what we know about father-child relationships is only about one-tenth of what we know about mother-child relationships because of researchers' focus on mothers. There is, however, a growing body of knowledge about father-child relationships that can help us understand more about fathers, mothers, and children.

FATHERS AND THEIR INFANTS

As noted in Chapter 1, fathers (and mothers) spend much more time with their children when they are infants, and the amount of time spent together decreases throughout the child's life. This pattern is counter to what many people assume, given that the stereotype is of a father who becomes interested in his children only when the children can be involved in team sports. The huge amount of time required to care for an infant often necessitates that both mothers and fathers devote many hours attending to the daily and nightly needs of an infant.

Contrary to popular opinion, mothers are not automatically more skilled at taking care of infants than are fathers. Child care skills are based on how much previous experience someone has with taking care of children. Since many women have had experience with child care duties, from babysitting when they were younger or from taking care of younger brothers and sisters during childhood, many new mothers feel more capable of taking care of an infant than many new fathers. However, new mothers and fathers who have equal previous experience with children show approximately equal levels of parenting skills. Often what happens is that even if the mother and the father are not sure of themselves with their first child, the mother takes on more of the parenting than does the father, and thus she develops more skills because of the additional experience. But if fathers stick with it, then they too can develop the same level of competence that mothers develop when they stick with it.[1]

As any parent knows, the parenting role has begun even before the child is born. In studies of married couples who planned the pregnancy, both fathers and mothers often report emotional attachment to the fetus. Parents' expectations during the pregnancy seem to be related to their experiences of the child even months after the birth. Regarding infant temperament, fathers and mothers who expected an "easy" baby (i.e., easy to soothe, cheery disposition, etc.) before birth tended to rate their 3-month-old baby as "easier" than did parents who expected a "difficult" baby. Similarly, fathers and mothers who expected a difficult child (i.e., a child who was difficult to soothe and who was rarely happy) tended to rate their 3-month-old as difficult. When objective observers rated these babies, the differences between the babies who were rated by their parents as more "easy" or more "difficult" were not that apparent from the observer's standpoint. In other words, it seems that fathers' and mothers' expectations of their baby's behavior has a great deal to do with how they later see their baby's behavior and only a little to do with the baby's actual behavior as seen by another person. This is not to say that difficult babies are not difficult. Anyone who has tried to soothe a colicky baby knows that it is not their imagination that is screaming its lungs out. It is to say, however, that our perceptions can sometime color the accuracy of our observations and that sometimes, getting an objective opinion can help us gain better perspective on a difficult situation.[2]

In addition to the interest in infant temperament, there has been a lot of interest in parent-infant attachment. There are primarily three types of attachment styles an infant can show with his or her parent or caretaker. I will use the term "parent" here for simplicity, but please note that these patterns can occur whether the primary caretaker is a biological mother, a biological father, a stepparent, an adoptive parent, a grandparent, an older sibling, or any other caretaker.[3]

Secure attachment is shown when the infant uses the parent as a secure base, seeks out the parent when upset, and seems upset when initially separated from the parent. This type of attachment is considered the most healthy type of attachment because it is associated with infants who grow up to be competent, happy, and curious children. Note that distress upon separation is not always a characteristic of securely attached infants and children, especially those infants and children who are in day care. I've heard more than one concerned parent comment on the ambivalence that they feel when their youngster seems so happy to leave them and go to day care or to see the babysitter. In these cases, as long as the infant or child is also pleased with seeking out the parents at other times, then the infant or child is still probably considered to have secure attachment to his or her parent. In addition, the parents can feel pleased that their child enjoys day care or the babysitter so much.[4]

Two types of attachment are considered problematic. Anxious resistant attachment occurs when the baby seems to go back and forth between seeking out contact with the parent and then resisting contact with the parent. Although this inconsistency can happen for most babies at some point, a baby who almost always shows this ambivalence with the parent would be considered to have an anxious resistant attachment with his or her parent. There is also an anxious avoidant attachment, which is characterized by a baby who seeks to be away from the parent and does not want to be reunited with the parent. Again, though this scenario may be shown by many infants and children at some time in their lives, an infant or child who shows consistent avoidance of a primary caretaker would be considered to have an anxious avoidant attachment with the parent. For most children, all three types of attachment show a relatively stable pattern of parent-child attachment from infancy through older childhood. In other words, if a child is securely attached to his or her parents at 3 months of age, then that child will probably be securely attached to his or her parents at 3 years of age and at 13 years of age.[5]

You may be surprised to learn that infants' attachment to their mother tends to be similar to their attachment to their father. That is, infants who are securely attached to their mother are most likely to be securely attached to their father. Infants who are insecurely attached to their mother (whether they are considered to have anxious resistant attachment or anxious avoidant attachment) are most likely to be insecurely attached to their father. This pattern seems related to the fact that most parental dyads tend to have similar parenting styles with their children, and these parenting styles seem to be most influential in determining the type of parent-child attachment.[6]

FATHERS AND THEIR YOUNG CHILDREN

There has been a great deal of interest in how fathers are different from and similar to mothers in their interactions with their preschool and school-aged children. In general, many commonalities exist between fathers and mothers, but there are some differences, as would be expected. Fathers and mothers tend to have similar developmental expectations and beliefs in disciplinary techniques with their pre-school children, but mothers report themselves to be more nurturing and more motivated to promote the child's mental health than are fathers. When parents are asked about what type of responses to children's behavior are acceptable, a number of differences emerge. Mothers report that they are much more accepting than fathers of positive reinforcement (e.g., praising a child for his or her good behavior) and response cost (e.g., taking a toy away from the child after he or she tried to break the toy). When compared with mothers, fathers report that spanking the child and getting medication to control a child's problematic behavior were more acceptable. Mothers and fathers did not differ in their ratings of acceptability of putting a child in a time-out chair. Given these differences, it is important that parents try to co-ordinate their responses to their children's behavior as much as possible. Children can learn appropriate behavior much more easily when both parents are united in the same goals and strategies for helping manage the child's behavior, even if the parents are in separate households.[7]

A primary difference between fathers and mothers is their involvement in playful activities with their children. As noted earlier, fathers spend a greater portion of their time with their children in play activities and mothers spend a greater portion of their time with their children in caretaking activities. These differences are maintained in early childhood and continue through middle childhood and the teenage years.[8]

One interesting area to consider is how children respond to their parents' warmth and acceptance. Warmth from both fathers and mothers is associated with children's greater likelihood of discussing their concerns with their parents. This suggests that if parents wish to keep an open dialogue with their children as their children progress from early childhood to the teenage years, both fathers and mothers need to establish a pattern of warmth and acceptance in order to allow their children to share concerns with them.[9]

With regard to intellectual development, fathers appear to have an influence on both sons' and daughters' intelligence, but there is a stronger connection between fathers' behavior and sons' intellectual development. For both sons and daughters, fathers' greater levels of involvement with their children is associated with higher intellectual functioning in their children. This association, however, is more pronounced for sons than for daughters. When fathers show higher levels of nurturing behavior with their sons and when fathers encourage their sons to master each task (rather than trying to intimidate their sons), the sons develop stronger cognitive and intellectual skills, especially in the sons' ability to analyze situations and to think critically. For daughters, the connections are more complicated. Fathers who show specific interest in their daughters' academic activities tend to have daughters with higher levels of intellectual and academic functioning, but some degree of autonomy and distance between father and daughter seems to be advantageous for daughters' intellectual development. In other words, it is not the case, as with boys, that fathers' greater involvement is associated with greater intellectual abilities in girls. Rather, how the father interacts with his daughter around these tasks is more important than how much time is spent in these tasks. Both fathers and mothers have been found to encourage their sons' achievement of tasks and to encourage their daughters' enjoyment of the activity rather than her completion of the task correctly. It may be that for both sons and daughters, parents' encouragement of task mastery and learning to solve problems is more highly associated with intellectual development than the encouragement of having fun. Of course, the best pattern might be to encourage both task mastery and the enjoyment of the problem-solving process in order for the child to develop high levels of intelligence as well as high levels of motivation toward learning.[10]

It should be noted that the majority of research into the father's role in children's intellectual development was conducted in the late 1970s and early 1980s. Since that time, there has been more attention to looking at paternal and familial influences in children's academic achievement in the school setting rather than in intelligence, per se. In general, both fathers' and mothers' warmth, involvement with their children, and high expectations of their children's success were associated with children's greater success in school. In one study, mothers' employment was more highly associated with children's academic achievement than was fathers' involvement with the children. Fathers and mothers with high educational and occupational goals for their children tend to have children with similarly high goals for themselves. These patterns have been found to be true for families from diverse ethnic, racial, and cultural backgrounds.[11]

Another important area of concern is whether fathers and mothers treat their sons and daughters similarly or differently. There used to be a strongly held notion that fathers differentiated between their children more than mothers. In other words, it used to be thought that fathers treated their sons and daughters much more differently than did mothers. More recently, sophisticated data analysis techniques known as meta-analyses, which combine the results of many studies, have helped clarify that there are actually very few differences between how fathers and mothers treat their sons and daughters. Overall, fathers and mothers seemed to treat their sons and daughters similarly when it comes to warmth, discipline, restrictiveness, encouraging achievement, and encouraging dependency. The primary difference in parents' treatment of their children was found in the encouragement of sex-typed activities (e.g., encouraging a son to play with trucks or to play football while encouraging a daughter to play with dolls or to play dress-up). Both fathers and mothers were found to encourage sex-typed activities for their sons and their daughters. Also, fathers were found to be more restrictive with their children than were mothers, but this was true for fathers' treatment of their sons as well as their daughters. This is another area in which there are more similarities than differences in the ways fathers and mothers interact with their children.[12]

FATHERS AND THEIR TEENAGERS

Many people automatically think of adolescence as a time of stress and stormy relationships within the family. Although this is the case for many families, most families with teenagers adapt quite well to the physical and social changes that are occurring for the teenager. It is estimated that 80% of teenagers make the transition from child to young adult without any major upheavals or problems during the teenage years. Although teenagers do have more variability in their moods than do younger children or adults (i.e., they have higher highs and lower lows with regard to how they feel), there does seem to be some predictability in these moods if you pay close enough attention to the teenager's patterns. As noted earlier, one way to make sure teenagers are able to share their concerns with their parents is to provide parental warmth and acceptance. Of course, the earlier parents start to develop a warm and trusting relationship with their child, the better. But it is never too late to try to improve the parent-child relationship, even in the teenage years.[13]

When fathers of teenagers were compared with fathers of younger children, fathers of teenagers reported more "task sharing" (i.e., working on projects together with the teenager) and more satisfaction with their role as a father than did fathers of younger children. It is not surprising, however, that teenagers and their parents do acknowledge that the teenage years can be difficult. When compared with fathers, mothers tend to feel that the teenage years are more difficult. Fathers and mothers of a teenage daughter think that the teenage years are more difficult than do fathers and mothers of a teenage son.[14]

A related area of interest for reseachers is to see how teenage sons and daughters feel about their father versus how they feel about their mother. Before puberty, boys felt lower attachment to their father than did girls, but after puberty, both boys and girls felt lower attachment to their father than to their mother. Although boys and girls felt the same level of warmth from both their father and their mother, boys and girls in the seventh grade reported that they felt closer to their mother than to their father. Teenagers of both genders report similar levels of identification with their mother, closeness to their mother, and involvement with their mother. But gender differences in teenagers are more evident in their relationship with their father. When compared with girls, boys felt greater involvement with their father and more identification with their father. Boys felt that they were punished more by both their mother and their father than did girls. Both boys and girls reported that mothers were more concerned about facilitating the teen's prosocial behavior (e.g., being kind, respectful, and responsible) than were fathers. When compared with boys, girls reported that their mothers were more encouraging for them to be empathic and nice. There were no such gender differences in teenagers' reports of their father.[15]

As would be expected, the parent-teenager relationship is associated with how teenagers feel about themselves. Teenage girls who feel that their father is warm and supportive and teenage boys who feel that their mother is warm and supportive are more likely to report feeling better about themselves; that is, they had higher self-esteem than their peers.[16]

FATHERS AND THEIR ADULT CHILDREN

As with other developmental stages, mothers continue to have more contact with their adult children than do fathers. Young adult daughters tend to feel closer to their mother than to their father, whereas young adult sons tend to feel equal levels of closeness toward their mother and their father. When the quality of the relationship is considered, young adult daughters tend to feel equally good about their relationship with their father and their mother, whereas young adult sons tend to feel better about their relationship with their mother than with their father. As would be expected, young adults who reported that their father and mother were warm and permissive were more satisfied with the parent-child relationship than young adults who reported their parents to be hostile and restrictive. In general, the ways in which fathers and mothers interact with their children continues to be different when their children reach adulthood. As in earlier developmental stages, fathers tend to share advice with their adult children, whereas mothers tend to offer emotional support to their adult children.[17]

When parents reach their elder years, there are some differences in their adult children's interactions with fathers and mothers. In studies of large, multiethnic samples of adults over the age of 65 and in studies of African American adults who were over 55 years of age, adults continue to show more contact with their mother than with their father. Older mothers receive more help with daily needs (such as household duties, transportation, and shopping) from their adult children than do fathers. It appears that the relationship between mothers and their adult children may be more reinforcing for both mothers and children than the relationship between fathers and their adult children. Specifically, higher frequency of contact with mothers was related to adult children's higher affection toward mothers and vice versa. For fathers and their adult children, more contact with fathers led to more affection toward fathers, but the reverse was not true (i.e., initial levels of affection toward fathers was not related to higher levels of contact with the father). These patterns of affection and contact are complex and obviously differ across families. As adults continue to live longer, more and more families will be faced with the challenges of having adult children care for their elderly parents.[18]

SUMMARY

In general, there are more similarities between the father-child relationship and the mother-child relationship than there are differences. Regardless of the age of the child, it seems that a parenting style known as "authoritative" is most conducive to raising children with good mental health. Fathers and mothers who are considered to have an authoritative parenting style show high levels of warmth and nurturance toward their children, but they also provide developmentally appropriate structure and control over their children. This type of parenting style is associated with fathers and mothers who set age-appropriate limits for their children and who are able to explain the limits to their children in a meaningful way. Overall, children whose parents are warm and affectionate but who expect socially appropriate behavior and who can give age-appropriate explanations for their expectations tend to have fewer behavior problems and better mental health than children raised by parents who are strict and who do not show very much warmth (a parenting style known as authoritarian), who are warm but who do not provide many limits or much structure (a parenting style known as permissive), or who show low amounts of warmth and low amounts of structure or control (a parenting style known as indifferent).[19]

Although there are many commonalities between fathers' and mothers' behavior and their relationships with their children, there are differences, namely, those that have been highlighted throughout this chapter. To complement what you have read here, interested readers can find a number of good books at the local bookstore or library that discuss different aspects of fathering; titles include *The Father Factor* by Biller and Trotter, *Fathering: Strengthening Connection with Your Children No Matter Where You Are* by Glennon, *The Joy of Fatherhood: The First Twelve Months* by Goldman, *Black Fatherhood: The Guide to Male Parenting* by Hutchinson, *Teen Dads: Rights, Responsibilities and Joys* by Lindsay, *Expectant Father* by Marshall, *How to Be a Pregnant Father* by Mayle, *The Passions of Fatherhood* by Osherson, *Fatherhood* by Parke, *The Measure of a Man: Becoming the Father You Wish Your Father Had Been* by Shapiro, and *The Father's Almanac—Revised* by Sullivan. For a fascinating account of how fatherhood in the United States has changed, you might want to read *Fatherhood in America: A History* by Griswold. For a poignant memoir that fluctuates between hilarity and the excruciating pain of being raised by an alcoholic father, *Dear Dad: Letters from an Adult Child* by comedian Louie Anderson should not be missed. Delightful and poignant accounts of what it is like to be a father in contemporary society are presented in *Fatherhood* by comedian, actor, and producer Bill Cosby, *Good Morning, Merry Sunshine* by journalist Bob Greene, and *Faith of Our Fathers: African-American Men Reflect on Fatherhood* by Andre Willis.[20]

In keeping with learning more about fatherhood, I would also encourage you to ask fathers you know about their experience of fatherhood. Whether the person you speak with is your own father or someone else's father, you can often learn a lot by asking men about their experiences as fathers and how those experiences are similar and different from the experiences of mothers. You might also make a point of talking to men with children of different ages to see what fathering was like many years ago compared with what it is like currently. Social expectations of fathering have changed throughout the years. For example, fathers used to be forbidden from participation in the hospital delivery room whereas their participation is expected within most segments of contemporary American society. Depending on the age of your children, you might also suggest to them that they interview adults of differing ages about what parenting was like at other times. One of my most treasured memories from grade school was the result of a history homework assignment to interview someone who had lived in the United States during the Great Depression. I was lucky enough to learn vivid stories from my grandmother, who talked about how hard she worked each day just to be able to buy a newspaper and how much joy she and her friends got from putting nails on the traintracks to see them smashed by the passing trains. This kind of oral history, which can be passed from generation to generation, is precious and is especially important to maintain so that we may understand the roles of children and parents through the ages. In addition to reading more about these topics, talk about these topics both within your family circle and outside of your family.

3

When Problems Develop in Children: Why Not Just Blame the Mother?

———•———

Few misfortunes can befall a boy which bring worse consequences than to have a really affectionate mother.

—W. Somerset Maugham

Go into any psychology department at any university in the country and chances are that you'll find at least one professor with a "Far Side" cartoon (by Gary Larson) posted on his or her door. Mr. Larson often communicates more about human nature in one cartoon than many psychology textbook writers cover in an entire chapter. One of the most telling cartoons in the Far Side series shows a client and a therapist in an office with lots of diplomas on the wall and a couch for psychoanalysis. The therapist is sitting calmly with paper and pen in hand. The client is sitting on the top of the coat rack and is wearing a clown hat, a trench coat, flippers, and a rubber duck swimming pool flotation device around his waist. The therapist is shown to be saying, "So, Mr. Fenton . . . let's begin with your mother."

Although this is an amusing and harmless cartoon, the message that rings through is that to understand deviant behavior, we must try to understand the client's mother. The phrase "mother blaming" has been used to describe the tendency for professionals and laypersons to blame mothers for children's problems. In her book *Don't Blame Mother*, Paula Caplan made the following observation: "If someone offered you a job saying 'If *anything* goes wrong, even sixty or seventy years from now, you will be blamed,' you'd tell them forget it. But that is what motherhood is" (p. 67). Although there is now more awareness about the harm of blaming mothers for their children's problems, a great deal of mother blaming (and father ignoring) continues to occur in psychological research and therapy. For these reasons and many others, a number of researchers have conceptualized mothering and fathering as feminist issues.[1]

HISTORY OF MOTHER BLAMING

A possible reason for the tendency to blame mothers is the idea of a "maternal instinct," which suggests that mothers are innately better than fathers at caring for their children and are therefore responsible for both good behaviors and bad behaviors exhibited by their children. You may be surprised to learn that the idea of a maternal instinct has been discredited for over 70 years. In 1923 a study was conducted with women who were about to give birth. They were asked, "Are you glad that you are going to have a baby?" The hypothesis was that a maternal instinct would be evident if the resounding answer was yes. Of the 87 mothers-to-be, 65 reported that they were not happy to be having a baby primarily because they could not afford the cost of raising another child or because they would have to discontinue their employment as a result of the birth of their child. These results were interpreted to suggest that there was no evidence for a maternal instinct. In 1926 this same conclusion was reached by the founder of behaviorism, J. B. Watson, who noted that new mothers who lacked experience with handling infants were often awkward and unskilled in the care of their own newborn. Since then a number of other studies have discounted the existence of a maternal instinct, and yet many people continue to believe in this myth.[2]

Another possible reason for mother blaming is a belief in the good mother/bad mother dichotomy. A number of writers have suggested that throughout Western cultures, mothers have been seen as all good or all bad, with little room for anything between. Based on current (and unrealistic) expectations, a good mother is aware of and able to fill every need of her child, is able to provide constant nurturance and care to her child, is always fascinated by her child, and is able to fill her role as a mother with no effort and no sense of self-sacrifice. Conversely, a bad mother is someone who is so concerned about her own needs that she ignores the needs of her child and is unaware of the harm she is constantly inflicting upon her child. This dichotomy leaves little room for the complexity of human behavior and, except in extremely rare cases, is completely unrepresentative of mothers' lives. Unfortunately, this dichotomy has led to a great deal of distress for many mothers who feel that even their best mothering efforts are never good enough. In addition, the myth of the good mother/bad mother dichotomy has ignored and invalidated the real work that goes into mothering.[3]

Ironically, the definition of good mothering (and conversely, bad mothering) has changed drastically throughout the ages. In ancient Sparta, mothers were expected to allow their weak or sickly infants to die—either by leaving the infant outside to die of exposure and starvation or by actively murdering the infant—to create a stronger and more hardy population. Mothers who did not take part in this practice were considered bad mothers and were ostracized socially by their neighbors and friends. Obviously, current standards in most countries would lead to public outrage if a mother murdered her child. However, there continue to be mixed messages about how mothers can live up to being good mothers.[4]

In her excellent series of sociological writings on the state of families, Jessie Bernard noted that mothers are provided with a no-win situation when it comes to expectations of being a good mother. For example, if a mother is overprotective and possessive about her child, she is seen as a less than adequate mother. Yet if a mother is somewhat independent from her child and if she does not dote on her child constantly, she is also seen as a less than adequate mother. Bernard argues that we must develop more realistic expectations for both mothers and fathers and that we should not blame mothers for their children's problems. Unfortunately, mother blaming has been pervasive not only in the community at large but also throughout the professional community, as is evident in theories of human development and clinical practice.[5]

MOTHER BLAMING IN PSYCHOLOGICAL THEORIES

Even without taking a class in psychology, most people know at least something about the theories of Sigmund Freud. Although Freud's early work discussed the importance of the father in the resolution of the Oedipal complex (where boys are thought to fall in love with their mother and see their father as a rival), the majority of Freud's work focused on the importance of the mother-child relationship in explaining normal and abnormal psychological development in children. Unfortunately, this focus on the mother-child relationship led to a great deal of mother blaming.

Other theorists followed Freud's lead and placed the responsibility of children's problems directly on the mother. Margaret Mahler suggested that childhood autism was the result of a maladaptive "state of symbiosis" between the mother and the child. Frieda Fromm-Reichmann suggested that schizophrenia was the result of a "schizophrenogenic mother" who was cold and domineering in the child's life. Other theorists took this idea one step further to argue that mothers of children who developed schizophrenia had put their children in a "double bind" by giving the child mixed messages of wanting to be close emotionally and then being emotionally distant when the child approached the mother. These theories have been discredited in more recent years.[6]

Ironically, one early series of studies could have been used to argue strongly against mother blaming; instead, it has been used to add to the belief in maternal culpability. In the mid-1950s, Harry Harlow and his colleagues at the University of Wisconsin wanted to study the importance of food versus the importance of physical contact on infants' attachment to their caretaker. Part of the interest in this area was that psychodynamic theorists such as Freud and Mahler argued that mothers had primary importance in their children's lives because of breast-feeding.[7]

To study this issue, Harlow and his colleagues took newborn monkeys and placed them in a cage with a wire-mesh "mother" surrogate and a terry-cloth "mother" surrogate. Sometimes the wire-mesh "mother" had a bottle attached so that the infant could feed, and sometimes the terry-cloth "mother" had the bottle attached. The researchers then observed which "mother" the monkey would spend more time with and which "mother" the monkey would seek when it was frightened. They found that regardless of which "mother" fed it, the infant monkey was more likely to spend time with the terry-cloth "mother" and to seek out the terry-cloth "mother" when it was distressed.[8]

Harlow and his colleagues used results from a series of studies like this to suggest that attachment between mother and child was related to the contact comfort that mothers provide, rather than to the food and sustenance they provide. Although these interpretations are accurate, these data could also be interpreted otherwise. Since breast-feeding was found not to be crucial in the attachment between caretaker and infant, these studies could have been used to show that the father-child relationship can be as equally meaningful as the mother-child relationship. Fathers as well as mothers can provide contact comfort. Thus, if the term "wire-mesh parent" and "terry-cloth parent" had been used in these studies, the results might have taken some of the responsibility from mothers and put the responsibility on both parents. Unfortunately, in psychology textbooks Harlow's studies continue to be referred to as studies of "mother love."[9]

MOTHER BLAMING IN CLINICAL RESEARCH

Given that theorists have directly or indirectly blamed mothers for their children's mental health problems, it is not surprising that researchers have followed in the same footsteps. Most researchers try to conduct research that tests some aspect of a theory. If the theory blames mothers, then the concomitant research will likely blame mothers. Unfortunately, this pattern has often been the case.

In a groundbreaking study, Paula Caplan and Ian Hall-McCorquodale reviewed research and therapy articles in professional journals that dealt with children's mental health problems. They wanted to determine whether mothers were more likely to be blamed for their children's problems than were fathers or other adults. In order to determine the changes in mother blaming over the years, they looked at articles published in 1970, 1976, and 1982. They found 125 articles appropriate for their review.[10]

In these articles, they found that the word "mother" was used a total of 2,151 times and the word "father" only 946 times. Mothers were discussed in clinical case study examples five times more than fathers (e.g., an example of a child client was given and the mother was described, but nothing was said about the father). Mothers' own psychological problems were said to be connected with their children's psychological problems in 64% of the articles, but fathers' own psychological problems were noted in only 34% of the articles. Overall, in 53% of the articles, some type of maternal culpability was given for children's mental health problems. Caplan and Hall-McCorquodale interpreted this information to suggest that mother blaming was quite evident in professional clinical journals. They also noted that the tendency to blame mothers did not change over the 12 years they reviewed (i.e., it did not decrease as some might have hoped) and that male and female professionals were equally as likely to blame mothers for children's mental health problems.

Unfortunately, Bruce Compas and I found relatively similar results in the years following Caplan and Hall-McCorquodale's review. We reviewed eight clinical research journals published from 1984 through 1991. We identified 577 research studies that included at least one parent and that investigated mental health problems in either the child or the parent(s) or both. Of these 577 articles, 48% included mothers in the study but did not include fathers, 1% included fathers in the study but did not include mothers, 26% included both mothers and fathers and provided data analyses for the mothers and fathers separately, and 25% either included "parents" without noting whether they were mothers or fathers or included some mothers and some fathers but did not provide separate analyses for mothers and fathers. Overall, this review suggested that researchers are still investigating the connection between mental health problems in mothers and their children more than in fathers and their children.[11]

Not surprisingly, this trend is also found in graduate students' dissertation research. After graduate students complete their dissertation research and earn their Ph.D., they can have the abstract summary of their dissertation published in *Dissertation Abstracts*, available at most university libraries. Louise Silverstein and I wanted to determine whether graduate students were more or less likely than established researchers to use mothers in their child-oriented research. We reviewed dissertations published from 1986 through 1994 and found that 59% of the studies included mothers only, 11% included fathers only, and 30% included both parents. When compared with established researchers, graduate students were more likely to use mothers only or fathers only in their child-oriented dissertation projects. It is interesting to note that the gender of the graduate student was related to whether or not mothers or fathers were central in their research. Male graduate students were more likely to include fathers in their dissertation research than were female graduate students. No other characteristics (type of doctoral degree, gender of advisor, or area of research) were related to the likelihood of including mothers or fathers in dissertation research. If graduate students are conceptualized as the professionals of the future, then the trend toward investigating mothers and ignoring fathers will remain unless significant changes are made.[12]

Although the actual investigation of mothers to the exclusion of fathers does not inherently mean that mothers will be blamed for their children's problems, researchers often draw conclusions that point to maternal culpability. Imagine you heard in a news report that severely anxious children have mothers who are more anxious than the mothers of children without an emotional problem. If no mention is made of the fathers of these children, it is impossible to know whether the fathers were included in the study and found to be no different from fathers of nonanxious children or whether fathers were not included in the study. If fathers were not included in the study, then to assume that only the mothers, but not the fathers, have problems with anxiety would be inaccurate. Unfortunately, when fathers are not included in studies, mothers are often inadvertently connected to their children's emotional and behavioral problems. These inadvertent connections can lead to mother blaming.

MOTHER BLAMING BY CLINICIANS AND THERAPISTS

Given that many theorists and researchers are also clinicians (and vice versa), it is not surprising to find that mother blaming is rampant in the clinical setting as well as in the research laboratory. Just as in research studies, fathers are often excluded from the therapeutic process. If therapists assess only the mother-child relationship, then they cannot learn anything about the father-child relationship, regardless of the father's presence or absence from the child's life. Stella Chess suggested that when the first series of questions has to do with the mother, "Other questions go unasked, hence unanswered" (p. 613). Therapists must be retrained to consider all aspects of the child's problems, including factors related to the child's father. One review of research on behavioral parent training found that fathers were included in only 13% of the families who received treatment.[13]

Although many clinicians feel that it is impossible to get fathers into the therapy room, other clinicians have argued that the origin of the problem may be in the therapist rather than in the father. For example, one clinical researcher chose to hold the first meeting, known as an intake session, with half the families in their own home; the remaining half met with the researcher in the clinic, which is standard procedure in most clinics. All families were then asked to attend the second session and subsequent therapy sessions in the clinic. The clinical researcher found that 43.5% of fathers who were initially met in the home attended the second session in the clinic. Only 6.5% of the fathers without the home visit attended the second session in the clinic. Although to argue that therapists should start making house calls for all their clients is unrealistic, these results do suggest that outreach of some kind is important if a therapist is committed to getting a father involved in a therapy session. One clinician found that if the father's participation in therapy was presented as "automatic" during the first phone call contact, then the fathers nearly always became involved in the therapy.[14]

When fathers do not participate in therapy, mothers are often blamed for not being able to get the child's father into the therapy session. One clinician argued that if the mother was not able to get the father into the therapy session, then the mother herself was not committed to therapy. Although this might be the case for some families, to blame the mother for the father's actions or lack of actions is unrealistic. Unfortunately, this blame of a mother for a father's actions is also evident in the professional literature on child sexual abuse. A number of authors have suggested that mothers are at least partially responsible for fathers who sexually abuse their children. Again, there may be some families for which this is the case, but no empirical evidence supports the claim that the mother is to blame for the father's incest.[15]

MOTHER BLAMING BY NONPROFESSIONALS

In addition to the investigation of mother blaming by professionals, there have been a number of studies that have investigated nonprofessionals' perceptions of maternal culpability. A study of college students was conducted to determine whether mothers, fathers, society, or the child itself was held more responsible for the child's emotional and behavioral problems. The researchers found that children were held most responsible for their own problems, followed by society, mothers, and then fathers. This study highlights the importance of considering perceptions of responsibility by someone (e.g., the child) or something (e.g., society) other than the mother or the father. When mothers and fathers were compared directly, mothers were considered to be more responsible for their children's emotional and behavioral problems than were fathers.[16]

To investigate these issues further, I conducted a similar study with college students, only I included problematic behaviors (such as arguing and drug use, which are referred to as externalizing problems), problematic emotions (such as depression and anxiety, which are referred to as internalizing problems), and healthy behaviors (such as doing well in school and having high self-esteem, which are referred to as adaptive behaviors). College students rated mothers as being most responsible for children's internalizing problems, fathers as being most responsible for children's externalizing problems, and both mothers and fathers as being most responsible for children's adaptive behaviors. These results suggest that perceptions of mothers' and fathers' responsibility for children's maladaptive and adaptive behavior are more complex than originally thought.[17]

The next issue to address is the possibility of mother blaming in families who are in therapy for their children's emotional and behavioral problems. By surveying mothers and fathers whose child is in therapy, researchers are able to investigate how much personal responsibility mothers and fathers feel for their child's problem behavior and how much they ascribe to the other parent or to other factors. Two different studies found remarkably similar results. Mothers and fathers were asked how much they felt responsible for their child's emotional and behavioral problems and then were asked how much responsibility the other parent had for their child's emotional and behavioral problems. Both studies found that mothers were more likely to take personal responsibility for their child's problems (i.e., they blamed themselves), rather than holding the child's father or other external sources responsible for their child's problems. Fathers tended not to take personal responsibility for their child's problems; rather, they tended to blame the child's mother for the child's problem.[18]

Given the mother blaming evident from many therapists, perhaps these parents learned either directly or indirectly from therapists that mothers should be held responsible for their children's mental health problems. It may be the case that in some of these families the mother's behavior was directly linked to the child's problems (e.g., an abusive mother or a mother who does not have adequate parenting skills). It is doubtful, however, that all families in both studies had mothers who were truly to blame for their children's problems and fathers who were truly blameless for their children's problems. Rather, it seems that parents whose children receive therapy blame the mother for the child's problem—regardless of the actual source of the child's problems.

PREVENTION OF MOTHER BLAMING

Many people might argue that the way to stop blaming mothers is to start blaming fathers. This solution would not be admirable or helpful. Mother blaming must be prevented in both the professional and the personal spheres. On the professional level, the first step is to acknowledge that there is a problem with mother blaming. Mother blaming has been so insidious in the professional community that many professionals are not even aware of it. Granted, some problems that lead to mother blaming are not initially intended to blame mothers (e.g., only investigating mothers of troubled children and not investigating fathers of troubled children, only asking about the mother-child relationship in therapy and not asking about the father-child relationship). It is of the utmost importance that professionals review their own behaviors to evaluate whether these behaviors directly or indirectly lead to blaming mothers for children's psychological problems.

A number of authors have begun pointing out these problems to other professionals. In addition to Paula Caplan and Stella Chess, whose writings have already been discussed, a few authors have made brief but pointed comments about mother blaming to alert other professionals to the problem. For example, in their well-known textbook of abnormal psychology Davison and Neale reviewed different theories of schizophrenia, and they added a footnote: "It is noteworthy that most theories implicating family processes in the etiology of abnormal behavior focus almost exclusively on the mother. Sexism?" (p. 396). In a review published in one of the premier journals in psychology, *Psychological Bulletin*, Geraldine Downey and James Coyne reviewed the research on children of depressed mothers and commented on the "mother bashing" often evident in this research. These examples illustrate what more authors should do when they encounter mother blaming in the professional literature.[19]

Another way for professionals and nonprofessionals to prevent mother blaming is to question sexist assumptions about what leads to mental health problems in children. For professionals, this means that they must question sexist theories that point only to mothers as the culprit in the development of children's mental health problems. It also means that they must begin to include both mothers and fathers in research regarding children's mental health problems. By definition, sexist research occurs when only one gender is investigated without any compelling reason for the exclusion of the other gender. Ironically, psychological and medical research has had a history of sexist research—but with the focus on men and boys rather than on women and girls. Several classic research studies that have been conducted on why people are motivated to achieve and how people develop moral behavior were conducted only with boys and men. In the medical field, most of the original studies that identified risk for heart attacks were conducted with males. The problem with this practice is that the results were applied to both genders, even though the results may have been accurate only for males. Only more recently have researchers questioned these series of studies and investigated these issues for males and females alike.[20]

Along with the need for professionals questioning of sexism and mother blaming in the professional literature, nonprofessionals must question sexist assumptions about parents that they hear from the media or in their own personal lives. When you hear about a study on the news that links mothers' behavior with children's problems, the first question you should raise is whether or not fathers were also included in the study. When you hear adult friends blaming their mother for their current problems, you should ask about their father's role in their life. For those of you who are mothers, when you find yourself blaming yourself for your child's problems, you should consider all the facets of the family environment, the social environment, and the child's genetic makeup that might have lead to your child's problems. The same is true for fathers who might automatically blame the child's mother for the child's problems.

It is also important for you to question your beliefs about your own mother's responsibilities in your life. In her book, *Don't Blame Mother*, Paula Caplan provides excellent suggestions for how to stop blaming your own mother. To begin with, she suggests that you humanize your image of your mother: Write a list of all the things your mother does, and then try to gain perspective on the ratio of her good versus bad behaviors; write your mother's biography to get a sense of her upbringing and the events that shaped her life before she had children; consider your mother's struggles; and find qualities to respect in your mother. She also proposes that you forge an alliance with your mother Consider the obstacles in forging this alliance regardless of whether the alliance can be attempted, confront your mother's power, and clarify your respective responsibilities. Further, you should choose and define a problem on which to start mending your relationship with your mother by only working on one problem at a time, remaining cognizant of the feelings that you have about the problem, and identifying the sources of the problem as well as of your feelings about the problem. Although these suggestions were developed to help mend the mother-daughter relationship, they will probably be useful to help mend any parent-adult child relationship.[21]

These strategies were suggested to prevent mother blaming, but the true solution to prevent mother blaming will be when we can move professionals and nonprofessionals away from blaming anyone for a child's problems. Looking for who is to blame rarely moves us in the direction of looking for solutions to the problem. It is therefore incumbent upon all of us to look forward for solutions rather than backward for blame.

As well as looking forward for solutions, professionals and nonprofessionals would be wise to look for similarities rather than differences between mothers and fathers. In most of the studies that you will read about in this book, more similarities than differences are found between mothers and fathers. In other words, characteristics of good, stable parents are similar for mothers and fathers. Although there are obviously some differences between women and men regarding the parenting role, to look for commonalities between mothers and fathers rather than always focusing on the differences between mothers and fathers will be less adversarial and less destructive.

A parallel issue has developed in the study of gender differences and gender similarities. If best-selling books such as *Men Are from Mars, Women Are from Venus* and *You Just Don't Understand: Women and Men in Conversation* are any indication, the general public has a hearty appetite to learn about the differences between women and men. It is not at all rare to hear people attribute the behavior of someone of the other gender to that person's gender (e.g., "All women are like that" or "What else can you expect from a man?). There has also been a long tradition in academia of investigating differences rather than similarities between women and men. In fact, a number of feminist psychologists have argued that the search for differences between women and men has been motivated by an attempt to allow inequality based on gender to continue. Because significant findings are more likely to be published than nonsignificant findings, another criticism of the research on gender differences is that it has been stacked in favor of reporting only differences between the genders. The term "the file drawer problem" has been used to describe the fact that for every published study that shows differences between men and women, there are probably a number of other studies that could not be published because no differences were found. These studies that fail to find differences between men and women are often stored away in file drawers.[22]

Even with the potential problem in publishing in professional journals only studies that show differences, a surprisingly small number of differences are consistently found between males and females. Of all the psychological characteristics that we can attribute to humans, only three gender differences are consistently found, and these differences are not all that substantial in size. Based on group comparisons in humans, males are found to have better quantitative abilities than females have (e.g., math abilities), males are found to excel in certain visual-spatial tasks when compared with females (e.g., a spatial perception task known as the rod-and-frame test, in which the participant is asked to line up a frame and a rod without any background cues to help orient him or her), and males are found to be more aggressive than females. These differences are encumbered by many caveats, which should be mentioned briefly. For example, when quantitative abilities are compared between men and women who have had equivalent math education, the gender differences disappear. This finding suggests that if girls and boys were equally encouraged to take math classes and were treated similarly in those classes, the gender difference in quantitative abilities would probably not exist. As for visual-spatial research, presentations of results of the rod-and-frame task have been criticized for presenting women in a negative light (i.e., as "field-dependent" and needing to have information from the background to be able to line up the rod and the frame) rather than in a positive light (e.g., as "field-sensitive" or "context-aware" and being astute to contextual cues that help orient the rod and the frame). In addition to this criticism, there are a number of other visual-spatial tasks that do not show consistent gender differences; these include, for example, complex spatial-visualization tasks that require the participant to mentally rotate objects as well as to perceive their spatial characteristics abstractly. With the differences in aggression that have been found, it is important to note that these differences are more obvious in childhood than in adulthood and that for most people, greater amounts of aggression are considered a problem rather than an asset.[23]

Having just focused on the differences between females and males, remember that a plethora of other psychological characteristics has been found to be comparable for females and males (e.g., intelligence, achievement abilities, and verbal abilities). As discussed in Chapter 2 about parenting, one of the most well established findings in psychological research is that regardless of gender, parents who are nurturant and who provide rationale structure to the child's life (the parenting style known as "authoritative") have children who are the most well adjusted. Thus, it appears that many parenting characteristics transcend the boundaries of gender to influence children in similar ways.

Acknowledging these similarities between mothers and fathers should help reduce mother blaming in our society.

One additional way to try to reduce and eventually to prevent mother blaming is to consider working toward greater gender equality within the family. Work within the family that has been traditionally carried out by women (e.g., childrearing, cooking, and cleaning) has a long history of being devalued in our society. Women are often expected to carry out these tasks even when they are employed full time. This practice is often referred to as the second shift, where women put in a full day at the office and then are expected to take care of everyone's needs at home. Women who are not employed outside of the home have often been referred to as "women who do not work" even though they are working 24 hours per day, 365 days per year, to keep the family functioning.[24]

SUMMARY

Overall, respect for mothers is ultimately tied to respect for women. A classic saying from the contemporary women's movement suggests that "the personal is political." When mothers find themselves doing the brunt of the housework and childcare in addition to paid employment, they may feel unsatisfied with their own lives, but they also realize that their lives are reflective of many women's lives. Some sociologists have argued that reaching equality in the workplace will be easier than establishing equality in the family because the workplace has more objective criteria than the home environment. If equality is to be sought in the home, it makes sense that the workplace would need to become more conducive to parents of both genders. The Family and Medical Leave Act is a step in the right direction, since these protections are given to workers regardless of their gender (e.g., both mothers and fathers can seek parental leave after the birth of a child). Writers in the contemporary men's movement have suggested that many men would like more of a role in their children's lives. If this is the case, then this would be a step in the direction of greater equality within the home and a step toward less mother blaming.[25]

4

WHEN PROBLEMS DEVELOP IN CHILDREN: WHAT ARE THE CHARACTERISTICS OF THEIR FATHERS?

———————————— ● ————————————

When you are living under the shadow of a great oak tree,
the small sapling, so close to the parent tree,
does not perhaps receive enough sunshine.

—RANDOLPH CHURCHILL
(son of Winston Churchill)

Whether in a college classroom or at a social gathering, one of the questions that I am asked most often when someone finds out that I am a clinical psychologist is, "What causes mental illness?" My usual answer is, "Do you have about a week to hear the answer?" The point is that there is no easy answer to what "causes" mental health problems and deviant behavior. Anyone who tries to convince you otherwise is ignoring the vast amount of conflicting evidence in the search for the "cause" of mental health problems. In fact, most researchers and theorists in this area do not even use the term "cause" (which is the reason that quotation marks are being used here). *Etiology* is the term used more frequently to help explain the different factors that lead to mental health problems. Researchers cannot argue that one factor "causes" another factor unless they can use certain research techniques, such as random assignment to different conditions, techniques usually not ethical in research on mental health problems. Anything short of this type of experimental method (or the identification of preexisting structural brain abnormalities) allows researchers to argue only that there is an association or a correlation between the development of a mental health problem and another factor.

For example, in Chapter 5 you will read that having a father who is depressed is associated with a number of emotional and behavioral problems for children. To be able to say that a depressed father "causes" mental health problems in his children, researchers need to be able to take a group of healthy infants and assign half of them to be raised by a depressed man and half of them to be raised by a nondepressed, psychologically healthy man. As interesting as the results of this study would be, this type of research can be completed only in the pages of a science fiction novel for obvious human rights and ethical reasons.

So, if we know that children of depressed fathers are more likely than children of nondepressed fathers to have emotional and behavioral problems, why can't we say that depressed fathers "cause" problems in their children? Well, it may be that a number of other factors are responsible for this association. For example, it may be that having a difficult child "causes" the depression in the father. It may be that another factor, such as conflict between the parents, "causes" the father's depression as well as the child's emotional and behavioral problems. Because these other factors may account for the connection between depression in fathers and problems in children, researchers cannot argue that paternal depression "causes" emotional and behavioral problems in children. Thus, in nearly all the research on fathers' and children's mental health problems, results are discussed in terms of associations and correlations rather than "causes."

If you've survived the lecture on research methods thus far, let me take you one step farther to explain the most promising theory of what leads to mental health problems in children as well as adults. In the past 20 years, there has been a great deal of interest in a theory known as behavioral genetics. At the root of this theory is the idea that many characteristics, including mental health problems, can be explained by a combination of genetic or biological factors and environmental or behavioral factors. One of the most exciting concepts that has developed out of the study of behavioral genetics is that the home "environment," which used to be considered the same for every child in the home setting, is now considered to be potentially different for each child in the family. In their book *Separate Lives: Why Siblings Are So Different*, Judy Dunn and Robert Plomin discuss the difference between shared environments and nonshared environments of siblings. Shared environment is the part of the family that is similar for all siblings in the household. For example, if the siblings grew up in the same house, with the same pets, and with the same food to eat, then these are the portions of the environment that were similar for each sibling. Nonshared environment is the part of the family that is different for each child in the family. For example, the older child may have been born at a time that the parents were not financially stable, whereas the younger child may have been born at a time when the parents were less stressed because they were more stable financially. Nonshared environment also includes characteristics such as being treated differently by parents, for example, when parents are more strict or more loving with one child in contrast to another. Dunn and Plomin argue that nonshared environmental factors have much more of an impact than shared environmental factors when considering the development of mental health problems in children.[1]

An example of what has been learned through the study of behavioral genetics can be illustrated when considering factors related to the development of schizophrenia in teenagers and adults. Given that schizophrenia is such a serious problem—the individual is often out of touch with reality, he or she may hear voices or see things that are not there, and he or she may not be able to care for him or herself—there has been a great deal of research in order to understand how the disorder develops and therefore how it might be treated or even prevented. As discussed in the last chapter, early theories of schizophrenia focused on blaming mothers for providing mixed messages of love and rejection toward their child. These theories have been discarded as a result of evidence from behavioral geneticists that schizophrenia develops from a combination of factors. Dunn and Plomin effectively illustrated the explanation of the development of schizophrenia by drawing a pie chart, with different pieces of the pie representing different factors that seem to lead to the development of the disorder. The largest piece (45% of the pie) represents nonshared environmental factors. The next largest piece (40% of the pie) represents genetic factors. An additional piece (10%) is not well understood and might be the result of statistical error, and the final piece (5%) represents shared environment.

To understand why schizophrenia develops, we must consider all those factors. For example, a child may be born with a heavy genetic predisposition toward the development of schizophrenia (e.g., both biological parents and all four biological grandparents were diagnosed with schizophrenia, to use an extreme example), but the child is raised in a stable and nurturing family environment by adoptive parents and does not end up developing schizophrenia. In contrast, a child may have a relatively low genetic loading for schizophrenia (e.g., one biological grandparent was diagnosed with schizophrenia), but the nonshared environmental factors with the biological parents (e.g., a great deal of communication problems in the family or a high level of negatively expressed emotion by both parents) are so strong that the child ends up developing schizophrenia in early adulthood.

This explanation should lead you to conclude that a number of factors are associated with the development of mental health problems. To further complicate the picture, different problems seem to be related to different factors. For example, schizophrenia, bipolar affective disorder (also known as manic depression), and attention deficit/hyperactivity disorder (AD/HD, also known as hyperactivity) seem to be more strongly linked to genetic factors than to other problems in mental health (e.g., major depression and post traumatic stress disorder). Given the complexity of this issue, it is important to keep in mind that most mental health problems are the result of numerous factors, and these factors often change over time. As mentioned earlier, these factors may also be reciprocal in nature (e.g., a challenging child may lead to less than admirable behavior in his or her parents, and the less than admirable parental behavior may lead to increased problem behavior in the child). For these reasons, the discussion of connections between mental health problems in fathers and their children will highlight the reciprocal nature of behavior within families, rather than trying to assign blame to any particular family member or personal characteristic.

This chapter focuses on children who have already developed problems and explores what the fathers of these children are like. A common research strategy is to identify a group of troubled children and a group of children who are not troubled and then compare the relevant characteristics of fathers of children in the two groups. Another research strategy is to identify two different types of troubled children and then compare the fathers of the children in these two different groups. In the majority of these studies, characteristics of mothers are usually evaluated (i.e., to compare the mothers of children in the different groups and to compare the mothers and fathers in the same groups).

Before beginning this discussion, I would like to explain the use of the word "nonclinical." Throughout the remainder of the book, I will often be describing studies of children diagnosed with a particular psychological disorder and children who have not been diagnosed with that disorder. Although it might be easiest to refer to the latter group of children as "normal," I have chosen not to use this terminology for a number of reasons. Children, teenagers, and adults who are diagnosed with a particular problem may be well functioning or "normal" in many other aspects of their lives. To imply that these individuals can be defined by the problems they are experiencing would seem harsh and inappropriate. Likewise, children, teenagers, and adults who are considered "normal" may in fact be experiencing difficulties in other aspects of their lives that are not the focus of the study. To be considerate of all these issues, I will use the term "nonclinical" to describe groups of individuals who are not experiencing the mental health problem being discussed.

Keeping in mind this terminology, let's dive into the literature on children and teenagers who are experiencing major psychological problems. The focus here will be on characteristics of the fathers of these children, but some attention will be paid to the mothers of these children. The current document used by psychiatrists, psychologists, counselors, and social workers to diagnose psychiatric disorders is known as the *Diagnostic and Statistical Manual of Mental Disorders–Fourth Edition (DSM-IV)*. This book is published by the American Psychiatric Association (APA) and was developed by a team of psychiatrists and psychologists. Where appropriate, *DSM-IV* terminology will be used. Specifically, discussed here will be fathers of children and teenagers who have problems with attention deficit/hyperactivity disorder, conduct disorder (CD) and delinquency, alcohol abuse, depression, anxiety disorders, schizophrenia, autism, and eating disorders.[2]

ATTENTION DEFICIT/HYPERACTIVITY DISORDER (AD/HD)

Attention deficit/hyperactivity disorder is one of the most common disorders in childhood. Many people refer to AD/HD either as attention deficit disorder (ADD) or as hyperactivity. The current *DSM-IV* uses the AD/HD terminology to acknowledge that there are different types of problems. Specifically, children, adolescents, or adults can be diagnosed as AD/HD—predominantly inattentive type (e.g., they have difficulty paying attention and concentrating), AD/HD—predominantly hyperactive-impulsive type (e.g., they are overly active and are very impulsive), or AD/HD—combined type (e.g., they have poor attention, difficulty concentrating, are overly active, and are impulsive). It is important to remember that diagnoses are appropriate only when the child or adult is significantly more inattentive or hyperactive than would be expected for someone of his or her age and gender. Many children and adults have high energy levels that they use to their advantage rather than to their disadvantage. For a diagnosis of AD/HD, the behaviors must be present in more than one setting (e.g., at home *and* at school), the behaviors must have been evident before the individual was seven years of age, and the behaviors must cause problems for the child, teenager, or adult in his or her academic, social, or occupational environments. A number of good books on the diagnosis and treatment of AD/HD in children and adults can be found in your local bookstore. In addition, Appendix A of this book lists organizations that help families of children with problems, including AD/HD.[3]

Based on studies of the general population of children in the United States, from 3% to 5% of school-aged children meet diagnostic criteria for AD/HD. Boys are much more likely than girls to meet diagnostic criteria for AD/HD, with estimates ranging from 3:1 to 9:1 boys to girls. Rates of gender differences are more pronounced in mental health clinics than in schools and in the community. In other words, not only are boys more likely than girls to be diagnosed with AD/HD, but boys who show problems are more likely than girls who show problems to be referred for mental health and psychiatric treatment. Many children who meet diagnostic criteria for AD/HD also can be diagnosed with oppositional defiant disorder (a disorder characterized by disobedience as well as oppositional behavior) or with conduct disorder (a more severe disorder that reflects a child's or teenager's severe rule violations such as stealing or fighting). Between 35% and 60% of children receiving mental health services for AD/HD also experience oppositional defiant disorder, and between 30% and 50% of children diagnosed with AD/HD eventually escalate their maladaptive behavior and can be diagnosed with conduct disorder. Overall, AD/HD is a widespread and serious problem that affects the children themselves, their families, their classmates, and their teachers.[4]

One way of understanding what leads to children's AD/HD problems is to ascertain if the parents of AD/HD children have problems. When fathers of AD/HD children are compared with fathers of nonclinical children, very few differences are found in psychological functioning but a few differences are found in personal and social characteristics. When compared with fathers of nonclinical children, fathers of AD/HD children felt worse about themselves and about their parenting skills, felt less hopeful about their child's behavior in the future, and had a shorter attention span. In contrast, fathers of AD/HD children do not differ from fathers of nonclinical children on a number of psychological characteristics (e.g., alcoholism, depression, criminal behavior, and perceptions of the family relationship). In other words, when fathers of children diagnosed with AD/HD are compared with fathers of children who are psychologically healthy, they exhibit very few differences in mental health and family functioning.[5]

Fathers of AD/HD children do, however, drink alcohol significantly more than do fathers of nonclinical children, although this greater amount of drinking is not reflective of alcohol abuse or alcoholism. Interestingly, these findings may be better understood in the context of a laboratory study conducted at Florida State University. To understand the impact of having to deal with an overly active child, researchers had college students over the age of 21 randomly assigned to deal with a hyperactive and difficult child or with a pleasant child. In actuality, the children in these two groups were the same—they were just coached to act either in a hyperactive and difficult manner or in a pleasant manner. Male and female college students were allowed to play with the child for about 18 minutes, and then they were allowed to drink as much nonalcoholic or alcoholic beverages as they wanted. They were told that the child would return in about 20 minutes to play with them some more. The researchers not only measured how much alcohol each student participant consumed but also asked participants to fill out questionnaires about their current mood and feelings.[6]

After interacting with a child who was acting hyperactive and difficult, both men and women reported greater distress and a worse mood than did men and women who interacted with a child who was acting pleasant. That is, both men and women seemed to feel much worse because of interacting with a hyperactive and difficult child. Because participants were randomly assigned in this study (i.e., each student had an equal chance of being selected to deal with a child who was acting hyperactive and difficult or a child who was acting pleasant), this experimental design allows the researchers to argue that the child's behavior "caused" the participants' changes in mood. Regarding alcohol consumption, women in the two groups did not differ in how much alcohol they consumed, but men did. Based on blood-alcohol level measurements, men who interacted with a child who was acting hyperactive and difficult drank significantly more alcohol than men who interacted with a child who was acting pleasant. This laboratory-based study gives us some indication that fathers of AD/HD children may show a greater likelihood of drinking alcohol as a way of dealing with their child's hyperactive and difficult behavior. Of course, the findings of this study should not lead people to think that drinking alcohol is a solution to dealing with hyperactive children. But the study does help us understand a little more about what fathers may be experiencing in reaction to their hyperactive children.

When fathers of AD/HD children were compared with fathers of children with other types of problems, some differences do emerge. For example, fathers of AD/HD children were more likely to themselves have experienced AD/HD in their childhood than were fathers of children with other types of problems. There were no differences between these two groups of fathers with regard to past criminal behavior or past abuse of illegal drugs.[7]

With regard to mothers, mothers of AD/HD children do not appear to drink more alcohol than mothers of nonclinical children, but they show greater levels of depressive feelings when compared with mothers of nonclinical children. When fathers and mothers of AD/HD children are compared with each other, few differences emerge. Specifically, fathers and mothers of AD/HD children did not differ in their feelings about themselves and their parenting skills, in their perceptions of family functioning, or in their attention span. In general, more hyperactive behavior was reported in children who had fathers and mothers who showed high levels of criticism and high levels of malaise or unhappiness.[8]

The few studies that have found differences between fathers and mothers of AD/HD children have shown that fathers drink more alcohol per week than mothers, mothers feel more depressed than fathers, and mothers feel more stress about their child's behavior than do fathers.[9]

Overall, there are few differences between fathers of AD/HD children and fathers of children who are not diagnosed with AD/HD. The differences that are evident, such as fathers drinking more alcohol and mothers feeling more depressed and stressed, may be reflective of what it is like to live with an overly active and impulsive child. One of the leaders in the investigation of AD/HD, Russell Barkley, suggests that although some parental characteristics can exacerbate AD/HD symptoms in children, most evidence points to genetic and biological reasons for the initial development of AD/HD in children.[10]

CONDUCT DISORDER AND JUVENILE DELINQUENCY

Conduct disorder is the diagnostic term for what most people think of as juvenile delinquency (JD). The term CD tends to be used in psychological and psychiatric writing, whereas JD is used in legal writing.

The *DSM-IV* diagnosis of CD is given when a child or adult consistently violates social norms and engages in activities that violate the basic rights of others. For example, a child who engages in stealing, fighting, and truancy would probably meet criteria for CD. Between 6% and 18% of boys can be diagnosed with CD and between 2% and 9% of girls can be diagnosed with the disorder. A person 18 years of age or older who continues to violate the rights of others can be diagnosed with antisocial personality disorder (APD). After the age of 18, approximately 3% of men and 1% of women can be diagnosed with APD.

Overall, delinquent behavior in youth is strongly connected with problematic behavior in their fathers. When compared with fathers of nonclinical children and with fathers of children diagnosed with other disorders, fathers of children and teenagers diagnosed with CD were more likely to be diagnosed as APD, to abuse alcohol, and to have overall higher rates of psychopathology. Interestingly, mothers of nonclinical children and mothers of children diagnosed with CD did not differ in their rates of anxiety disorders. Delinquent behavior in teenagers is associated with fathers who communicate in a defensive and unsupportive manner, who show low levels of supervision of their children's activities, and who have a poor relationship with their teenager.[11]

Children's and teenagers' level of aggression also appears to be associated with their father's level of physical aggression. When compared with nonclinical youth and youth diagnosed with nonaggressive disorders, delinquent teenagers, adjudicated male teenage offenders, homicidally aggressive children, and teenagers who ran away from home were more likely to be physically abused by their father. A troubled father-child relationship is also associated with levels of extreme violence, such as rape and murder of one's own parent.[12]

Mothers of children and teenagers diagnosed with CD also show greater levels of psychopathology and abusive behavior than do mothers of nonclinical children and teenagers. When compared with mothers of nonclinical children, mothers of children diagnosed with CD were more likely to abuse alcohol and drugs. When compared with mothers of children diagnosed with other disorders, mothers of children diagnosed with CD were more likely to be diagnosed with APD or major depression. Overall, fathers' and mothers' delinquent and aggressive behaviors were associated with the delinquent and aggressive behavior of their sons. There is conflicting evidence, however, as to whether mothers' behavior or fathers' behavior is more important in the development of conduct problems in children. It appears that fathers' parenting may be more connected to conduct problems when the conduct problems are extreme enough to require therapy for the child, but that mothers' parenting may be more connected to conduct problems that are not as extreme.[13]

Because CD is more prevalent in boys than in girls, the majority of research has been conducted with boys. The few studies that have included girls diagnosed with CD have lead to conflicting findings. One study suggested a stronger connection between girls' CD behavior and their mothers' rather than their fathers' behavior, but two other studies found that both boys and girls diagnosed with CD were alike heavily influenced by both their father's and their mother's behavior. Given these conflicting findings, whether delinquent behavior involves stronger mother-daughter connections or father-son connections is unclear.[14]

It is important to note that CD and delinquency seem to be associated with a combination of risk factors, rather than with just one risk factor alone. The combination of poor parenting, parental uninvolvement, parental criminality, parental aggressiveness and abuse, and deviant peers is highly associated with delinquency in children and teenagers. Poor discipline, parental absence, low socioeconomic status, and poor parental health do not appear to be directly related to delinquency in youth. There is some indication that father absence or mother absence is associated with minor offenses but not with serious offenses in teenagers. Given the serious ramifications of CD and delinquent behavior, it is important to help fathers and mothers change their own behavior in order to prevent their children from developing such serious and problematic behaviors.[15]

ALCOHOL ABUSE

Ironically, research on the fathers of children and teenagers who abuse alcohol is scarce. Since there is almost no research on fathers of children and teenagers who abuse other substances, only alcohol abuse will be covered in this section. According to *DSM-IV*, alcohol abuse is diagnosed when a chronic and harmful pattern of alcohol use interferes with personal functioning and leads to personal, social, medical, or legal problems. Although there are children and teenagers who abuse alcohol, the average age of the onset of alcohol abuse is 23.2 years. For this reason, most studies that have investigated the connection between fathers and alcohol abuse in their children have actually focused on children who are already grown. Studies that focus on adults and then have them report on their childhood are referred to as "retrospective" studies because the adults are asked to think about their own childhood and report how they remember being treated as a child. This method of research entails some problems. How adults feel at present can influence how they remember their childhood, with more troubled adults, for example, recalling more troubled childhoods even when indications from other sources prove otherwise. However, in a thorough study of retrospective studies, retrospective reports were found to be valid for the most part.[16]

Based on retrospective studies, young adult men and women who are alcoholic were more likely to have an alcoholic father than to have an alcoholic mother. In fact, there appears to be a strong genetic connection for alcoholism between fathers and sons. For boys and girls alike, the combination of parents who abuse alcohol and parents who are perceived to be permissive toward alcohol and drug use, growing up in extreme poverty and expressing delinquent behavior were associated with the development of alcohol abuse in teenagers and young adults.[17]

Although the onset of alcohol abuse does not usually occur until young adulthood, this area is in need of further research to find out how fathers and mothers influence children and teenagers as they are growing up. Results from such studies may help us find ways to prevent children and teenagers from eventually abusing alcohol and from possibly harming themselves and others in the process.

DEPRESSION

Depression, formally known as major depressive disorder, is diagnosed when children or teenagers experience at least a two-week period of depressed mood or loss of interest in things they used to enjoy and when they experience a number of other symptoms, such as being very restless or fidgety, having a disturbed pattern of eating, having a disturbed pattern of sleeping, feeling worthless, and wanting to be dead. Approximately 7% of children and teenagers can be diagnosed with major depressive disorder at any one time. Before puberty girls and boys are about equally likely to be depressed, but after puberty girls start showing higher rates of depression than boys. In adulthood women are approximately twice as likely to be depressed as men. With regard to children and teenagers, in addition to the 7% of children who can be diagnosed with depression, 5% of children and teenagers show elevations in depression that are referred to as a depressive syndrome and between 10% to 20% (based on parents' reports) and 20% to 40% (based on teenagers' self-reports) could be said to have a depressed mood at any one time.[18]

Surprisingly few studies have looked at the connection between fathers and children or teenagers who are depressed. These studies reveal conflicting evidence as to the connection between childhood depression and fathers' behavior. For example, fathers of depressed children were no more likely than fathers of nondepressed children to experience many types of psychopathology. One study did find that fathers of depressed children were more likely to be diagnosed with APD than fathers of nondepressed children. There does appear to be a stronger link between mothers' and daughters' depression than between fathers' and sons' depression.[19]

In contrast, a few studies have found a strong connection between fathers' behavior and children's depression. Having a poor or conflicted relationship with their father is associated with depression in children and teenagers. Thus, there is some indication that a troubled father-child relationship is connected with childhood depression, but there are indications that the connection is stronger for a troubled mother-child relationship and depression in children and teenagers.[20]

When retrospective reports of the father-child relationships are provided by adults who are depressed, a more clear connection between fathers' behavior and children's depression emerges. Relatively consistently, adults who are depressed are more likely than nondepressed adults to report that their father had experienced a psychiatric problem and that their father showed poor parenting by evidencing low levels of affection and love combined with high levels of control.[21]

Taken together, these two research methodologies suggest some connection between the father-child relationship and depression, but there may be a stronger connection for adults who are depressed in contrast to children who are depressed. In addition, there may be a somewhat stronger connection for mother-daughter depression than for father-son depression. Given that depression is more prevalent in teenage girls and in women, this greater connection between mothers' and daughters' depression is not surprising.

ANXIETY DISORDERS

A number of disorders are combined under the heading "anxiety disorders." Problems such as panic disorder with or without agoraphobia, specific phobias, social phobias, obsessive-compulsive disorder (OCD), generalized anxiety disorder, separation anxiety disorder, and post traumatic stress disorder can be diagnosed for children and teenagers. Unfortunately, very few studies in this area have investigated the fathers of children with an anxiety disorder. The few studies that have been conducted suggest a tentative connection between anxiety disorders in children and problematic functioning in fathers.

For example, when compared with nonclinical children, children diagnosed with OCD were more likely to have a father who showed obsessional thought patterns and were more likely to have a father who was diagnosed with OCD himself. In contrast, children who experienced panic disorder had fathers who were no more likely to be diagnosed with a panic disorder than the fathers of children who had not experienced a panic disorder. Fathers of children who experienced a variety of anxiety disorders were no different than fathers of nonclinical children to be diagnosed with APD or alcohol abuse.[22]

Unfortunately, this area of research is fraught with holes in what has been studied and only tentative conclusions can be drawn from what is presently known. Additional research is needed to investigate fathers of children with different types of anxiety disorders and then separate comparisons will need to be completed for these different problems. Only then can more substantial conclusions be drawn.

SCHIZOPHRENIA

Schizophrenia is a serious disorder characterized by a lack of being in touch with reality and a lack of ability to take care of one's own basic needs. Seeing or hearing something that does not in fact exist (which is known as a hallucination), believing something that is not accurate (which is known as a delusion), and having feelings that are not common (such as blunt or no affect or very changeable and labile affect) are all symptoms of schizophrenia. For a child to experience schizophrenia is rare indeed. Most men who experience schizophrenia have their first psychotic break, that is, the first time they show symptoms, in their mid-20s, and women usually experience their first psychotic break in their late 20s. For this reason, almost all studies completed about fathers with schizophrenic offspring are conducted with adults who are diagnosed with schizophrenia.

As mentioned earlier, a strong genetic loading is associated with the development of schizophrenia. Certain characteristics within the family environment are, however, associated with the development and maintenance of the disorder. Fathers who showed high levels of hostility, severe discipline, and overprotection had adult children diagnosed with schizophrenia who showed greater symptoms and less improvement in therapy. For fathers and mothers alike, poor communication patterns and many negative emotional expressions were associated with greater likelihood of the development of schizophrenia. Overall, the combination of genetic risk and problematic parenting by fathers and mothers can put offspring at risk for the development of schizophrenia.[23]

AUTISM

In the past, childhood schizophrenia and childhood autism were confused. These two disorders are now considered to be distinct. Although both disorders are characterized by a lack of being in touch with reality, the disorders are quite different. In contrast to schizophrenia, which does not usually occur until early adulthood, autism is almost always evident from very early childhood and is sometimes evident in infancy and toddlerhood. Although relatively rare, autism is a severe disorder. Autistic children usually have difficulty establishing social relationships, and they often appear out of touch with their social surrounding. Autistic children also often show unusual behavior, known as stereotyped movements (e.g., hand flapping or repeated movements without any apparent purpose).

Although there is a history of blaming parents (especially blaming mothers) for their children's autism, strong evidence suggests that autism is in no way attributable to mothers' or fathers' behavior. Studies in England and the United States suggest that fathers and mothers of autistic children do not differ from fathers and mothers of nonclinical children. As may be expected, having a child who is autistic is associated with higher rates of parenting stress. Appropriately, the field has moved away from trying to find ways parents have "caused" autism in their children and toward trying to find ways to help these parents and their children.[24]

EATING DISORDERS

Awareness of eating disorders has increased significantly over the decade. There are two primary types of eating disorders, both of which are relatively rare. Anorexia nervosa, characterized by limited food intake and unrealistic expectations about how thin one should be, is evident in approximately 1% of the population. Bulimia nervosa is characterized by binge-purge episodes where extreme amounts of food are ingested and then extreme measures are taken to purge the food, usually through use of laxatives or self-starvation or exercise. Bulimia is evident in approximately 3% of the population. More than 90% of people with these eating disorders are girls or women.

Although full-blown eating disorders are relatively rare, many girls and women have subthreshold levels of eating disturbance and body image disturbance. There is such widespread self-dissatisfaction with girls' and women's bodies that the term "normative discontent" has been coined to reflect how females feel about their body. A great deal of research points to sociocultural influences that may lead to girls' and women's dissatisfaction with their body. For example, girls and women are often inundated with media images of models who are actually significantly underweight. In addition, a number of print ads, commercials, and now movies use airbrush and computer techniques to present women's bodies in an unrealistically thin or toned manner.[25]

Add to these sociocultural influences a number of studies that have explored the link between the father-daughter relationship and daughters' eating disorders. Because eating disorders are often not evident until older adolescence and young adulthood, many of these studies are retrospective in nature.

Unfortunately, the results of these studies are complicated; they do not provide a clear-cut picture of the relationship between fathers and daughters when the daughters develop an eating disorder. Based on daughters' reports, the most consistent findings suggest that fathers of daughters with an eating disorder show less love and care for their daughters when compared with fathers of daughters without an eating disorder. It also appears that fathers of daughters with anorexia were less emotionally involved than were fathers of daughters without an eating disorder. However, when compared with fathers of daughters with another type of psychiatric problem, fathers of daughters with an eating disorder actually look pretty good in their fathering abilities. Specifically, when compared with fathers of teenagers with a psychiatric disorder, fathers of teenagers with an eating disorder showed higher rates of love and care. Taken together, these results suggest that according to daughters' reports, fathers of daughters with an eating disorder provide less love and care than fathers of nonclinical daughters, but they give more love and care than fathers of daughters with another type of psychiatric disorder.[26]

When considering problematic eating attitudes that have not led to an eating disorder in adolescent girls, the father-daughter relationship does appear to be important. One study found that girls with maladaptive eating attitudes reported greater problems in their autonomy from their father and in problem solving with their father than did girls with adaptive eating attitudes. In addition, girls with maladaptive eating attitudes reported problems communicating with and sharing warmth with both their father and their mother. Investigation of problematic eating attitudes is important because such attitudes can be a precursor to the development of more serious eating disorders.[27]

Interested readers are referred to a book that explores the clinical issues in working with families in which a daughter has an eating disorder. Margot Maine wrote her book *Father Hunger: Fathers, Daughters and Food* with an eye toward helping change the father-daughter relationship in order to alleviate the eating disorder in the daughter.[28]

SUMMARY

In general, fathers of children with a psychiatric diagnosis differ from fathers of children without a psychiatric diagnosis. Although there are stronger connections for some disorders (such as alcohol abuse) than for others (such as depression), the father-child relationship appears to influence and in turn to be influenced by a child's psychological problems. In relation to mothers, there appear to be more similarities than differences in the father-child and mother-child relationship with regard to children and teenagers who are experiencing problems. As mentioned in Chapter 2, parenting that is characterized by warmth and rationale structure is associated with fewer mental health problems in children and teenagers. In some cases, this authoritative parenting style may help prevent children from developing psychological problems, even if there is a genetic predisposition toward these problems.

5

When Fathers Have Problems: What Are the Characteristics of Their Children?

•

If there is anything that we wish to change in the child,
we should first examine it and see whether it is not
something that could better be changed in ourselves.

—Carl Gustav Jung

Imagine that a baby girl is born into a family in which both parents are severely depressed. That baby not only has possible genetic loading toward depression but also may experience parenting that is not conducive to growing up in a psychologically healthy manner. For example, as she learns to smile and squeal, her parents may not respond at all and most probably do not respond with the delight and smiling joy with which many better-functioning parents would respond. Now, consider that this baby girl spends a lot of time with her grandparent, who used to be depressed but who is now psychologically healthy. The grandparent's behavior may serve to protect the baby from the depressive and somber environment that is provided by her parents. Conversely, imagine that the baby has no other caretakers and has been exposed only to a joyless existence. Most probably she would grow up to experience psychological problems at least partly the result of a depressive environment.

As explained at the beginning of Chapter 4, we do not investigate fathers and mothers with problems to see what problems they "cause" in their children. Rather, we explore fathers and mothers with problems in order to determine what characteristics in the fathers and mothers are associated with difficulties in their children. Much of the research in this area has attempted to identify the factors that put children at risk for developing mental health problems (factors such as having a parent who is experiencing psychological problems) and the factors that seem to protect children from developing mental health problems even in the face of very adverse circumstances (factors such as having a well-functioning caretaker).

Before diving into the risk and protective factors that are specific to fathers and their children, it is worthwhile to consider risk and protective factors that have been well established through long-term research projects. One of the most ambitious and well-respected studies of risk and protective factors has been conducted by Emmy Werner from the University of California at Davis. This study has continued for over 35 years. In 1955 Werner and her colleagues collected information on 698 children who were born on the island of Kauai in the Hawaiian Islands. These children have been followed by Werner and her colleagues ever since that time. The point of this research has been to identify factors in the children's lives that would put them at risk for developing problems and also to identify factors that seemed to protect them from developing problems. From the initial group of children, 30% of infants were considered to be at high risk for the development of problems because they experienced stress or trauma before, during, or immediately after being born or because they were born in chronic poverty or because they lived in a family with a great deal of problems (such as having parents who argued constantly or having a parent with a mental disorder or having parents who were divorced). By the age of 18, two-thirds of these infants went on to develop significant problems, including behavior disorders, delinquency, and teen pregnancy, but one-third developed into well-adjusted young adults. The one-third of the children who did not develop problems, even in the face of adverse surroundings, are referred to as "resilient" children.[1]

The main goal for Werner and her colleagues was to find out what characteristics seemed to protect these resilient individuals from being negatively influenced by adverse environmental factors. They identified a number of protective factors that can be categorized into three areas: protective factors within the individual, protective factors within the family, and protective factors within the community. Protective factors within the individual include having an easy temperament as an infant, having good communication and problem-solving skills as a young child, having a special interest or hobby from which the child can gain a sense of pride, having at least average intelligence, having an internal locus of control (i.e., the child feeling that he or she can effectively have control over his or her own life), and having a positive sense of oneself (i.e., good self-esteem). Protective factors within the family include having at least one stable caregiver with whom to form a close emotional bond (this person is often a grandparent or an older sibling), having religious beliefs that help the family find comfort and meaning during difficult times, and for boys, coming from a family that supports emotional expressiveness while maintaining structure that is often provided by a male model (such as a father, grandfather, uncle, or older brother), and for girls, coming from a family with a reliable female caregiver (such as a mother, grandmother, aunt, or older sister) who emphasizes independence and challenging oneself. Protective factors within the community included having a stable and caring role model outside of the family (such as a teacher or an elder within the community) and later having the chance to become involved in adult educational opportunities or having a supportive and close friend or romantic partner.

In addition to examining these global risk and protective factors, a number of researchers have investigated the risk factor of having a father with psychological problems. In general, having a psychologically distressed father or mother puts children and teenagers at risk for the development of a psychological problem. However, the specific types of problems children experience depend on the type of psychological problem the parent experiences. Fathers' primary problems that are covered here are APD/criminality, alcohol abuse, depression, anxiety disorders, schizophrenia, physical abuse, and sexual abuse.

ANTISOCIAL PERSONALITY DISORDER/CRIMINALITY

As noted in Chapter 4, an individual aged 18 or older who chronically violates the rights of others and who has done so since at least age 15 can be diagnosed with APD. Antisocial personality disorder is considered a long-standing personality problem. In addition to violating others' rights, APD individuals often lack remorse about these violations; in other words, they do not feel sorry for their misdeeds. Often they show a high degree of deceit and impulsivity in dealing with others. Approximately 3% of men and 1% of women meet diagnostic criteria for APD. There is a large overlap between the diagnosis of APD and taking part in criminal behavior.

Given the importance of knowing about fathers who have criminal problems, it is surprising to find that very little research exists in this area. Although a great deal of research has shown a connection between juvenile delinquency in youth and criminality in fathers, this research has almost exclusively been conducted with children and teenagers who are already behaving in a delinquent manner (see Chapter 4 for review). Although this method of research is quite useful, it is also important to find a group of fathers who are engaged in criminal activities and then see how their offspring are functioning. It may be that many of their offspring are functioning well as a result of other factors, such as a stable mother or a strong social network. One study explored Danish teenagers who were at risk for problems because of their father's criminal behavior and compared those teenagers who had gotten caught for criminal activities with those teenagers who had apparently not engaged in criminal activities. Those teenagers who had not been caught for illegal activities had significantly higher intelligence than those teenagers who had been caught for illegal activities. As mentioned earlier in this chapter, it appears that intelligence may have served as a protective factor to prevent the deleterious effects of having a father who breaks the law. An alternative conclusion, however, is also possible. It may have been that brighter teenagers were able to conduct their criminal activities in such a way as to avoid being caught and prosecuted. Given that legal records were used in this study to determine the criminal behavior of the youth, it is possible that other factors are responsible for the findings.[2]

Other than the study just discussed, the only other child-oriented studies of fathers who have problems with criminal behavior are studies in which fathers in jail or in prison are studied to see what type of contact they have with their children. Unfortunately, these studies address not the children's well-being but, rather, the well-being and wishes of the fathers who are incarcerated. Nonetheless, these studies are helpful in understanding what it is like to be a father behind bars.

Based on a study of over 300 fathers incarcerated in a maximum-security prison, it appears that the majority of fathers had some contact with their children. Approximately 30% of the fathers said that their children visited them at least once or more per month, 37% said that they saw their children less than once a month, and 33% said that they had no face-to-face contact with their children since being in prison. The overwhelming majority of fathers in the study reported that they had other forms of communication with their children. Approximately 77% said that they received mail from their children, 85% said that they had sent mail to their children, and 78% said that they had spoken by phone with their children. Fathers who had lived with their children before being jailed were more likely to be visited by their children and to speak on the phone with their children. Living situations before the father's incarceration were not related to mailing letters between fathers and their children once the fathers were in prison.[3]

Another study of fathers in a maximum-security prison suggested that fathers were interested in receiving education on how to become a better parent. A total of 91% of fathers reported that they would like to learn how to improve their parenting skills. Men in the same maximum-security prison who did not yet have children also reported that they would like to learn more about parenting. A total of 65% of the nonfathers in this prison reported that they would like to learn how to be a good parent in case they had children once they left prison. Given that most of these men would eventually be released from prison and possibly have a caretaking role in their children's lives, these results suggest that parenting classes for men in prison would be well received and could be quite useful.[4]

The next obvious step in this line of research is to find out how father-child contact influences the child's well-being when the father is in jail or in prison. It would not be surprising to find that such contact is helpful for some children and harmful for other children, depending on the father-child relationship, the mother-father relationship, and the mother-child relationship.

ALCOHOL ABUSE

Nearly everyone knows someone who has a problem with alcohol. For the official diagnosis of alcohol abuse, a person must have a problematic pattern of alcohol use that interferes with personal functioning and leads to problems in the personal, social, medical, or legal arena. Approximately 5% of adults meet the strict definition of alcohol abuse.

The study of fathers who abuse alcohol is unique because this is perhaps the only area in which fathers are studied to the near exclusion of mothers. Men are two to three times more likely to be dependent on alcohol than are women. Although men, and therefore fathers, are much more likely to abuse alcohol than are women, and therefore mothers, there is almost no research on children of alcoholic mothers. Given the recent popular interest in adult children of alcoholic parents, the research literature on adult children of alcoholic fathers will be discussed after the research literature on younger children of alcoholic fathers is discussed.

Relatively consistent evidence indicates that children of alcoholic fathers have more psychological, behavioral, and social problems than children of fathers who do not have any psychological problems. More specifically, when compared with children of fathers without any psychological or psychiatric problems, children of alcoholic fathers show greater levels of alcohol and drug abuse, conduct problems, hyperactivity, depression, anxiety, and personality problems. Children of alcoholic fathers also experience greater levels of family stress and poor discipline practices than do children of psychologically healthy fathers. One study even looked at where the father did the majority of his drinking to see if drinking in the home around the children was more harmful than drinking away from the home. This study found that no matter where the father did the majority of his drinking, his children were at increased risk for psychological problems.[5]

Note that there are stronger links for alcohol abuse between fathers and their sons than between fathers and their daughters. There is support for the idea that alcohol abuse is heavily genetically predetermined and that the link seems to be through the Y chromosome (from father to son) rather than through the X chromosome. Even with this strong genetic linkage, however, it is important to note that not every son of an alcoholic father goes on to abuse alcohol himself. Approximately 30% of sons of alcoholic fathers go on to abuse alcohol themselves in adolescence or adulthood. The overwhelming majority of sons of alcoholic fathers (70%) do not go on to abuse alcohol themselves.[6]

In addition, not every study finds differences between children of alcoholic fathers and children of psychologically healthy fathers. It appears that teenagers of alcoholic fathers do not differ from other teenagers in their school attendance and their grade point average. Also, when children who are already experiencing problems are compared to those who do or do not have an alcoholic father, few differences are found in personality and brain functioning. Aside from these few studies, there is consistent evidence that children and teenagers of fathers who abuse alcohol show more problems than children and teenagers of fathers who are psychologically healthy.[7]

Even though there are consistent differences between children of alcoholic fathers and children of psychologically healthy fathers, it is important to note that these differences may not be unique to children of alcoholic fathers. When children of alcoholic fathers are compared with children of fathers who are depressed or who are suffering from schizophrenia, few differences emerge. In other words, it appears that having a father with any psychological or psychiatric problem such as alcohol abuse, depression, or schizophrenia is associated with mental health problems in children and adolescents.[8]

Similar patterns are apparent when adult children of alcoholic fathers are explored. Adult children of alcoholic fathers (ACOAs) show more alcohol abuse, mental health problems, and personality problems than do adult children of psychologically healthy parents. These differences, however, are not as prevalent when ACOAs are compared with adult children of fathers who experience some other psychological problem.[9]

Since much of this research has been completed on male offspring of alcoholic fathers, it is important to realize that women who abuse alcohol seem to be equally influenced by alcohol abuse in their father or in their mother. When adult women of alcoholic fathers escape problem drinking for themselves, they are still somewhat more likely to marry a man who abuses alcohol.[10]

The issue of romantic relationships in adult children of alcoholic fathers has received a great deal of attention in the popular press within the past few years. Unfortunately, there are few well-controlled studies that have explored these patterns in a rigorous scientific manner. One study that did explore psychological functioning and romantic relationships in adult daughters of alcoholic fathers was conducted by Carole Giunta and Bruce Compas in Vermont. Contrary to what is often discussed in the popular press and on daytime talk shows, adult daughters of alcoholic fathers did not show greater problems with fear of intimacy or greater psychological problems when compared with adult daughters of psychiatrically disturbed fathers or with adult daughters of psychologically healthy fathers. Similar results were found for adult daughters of mothers who abused alcohol. This well-designed study suggests that there may be more similarities between adult daughters of alcoholic or distressed parents and adult daughters of healthy parents than previously thought.[11]

Overall, young children and adult children of alcoholic fathers seem to be at risk for the development of more psychological problems than young children and adult children of fathers who have not experienced any psychological problems. This greater risk for problems, however, seems similar to the risk that is experienced by young children and adult children of fathers with other types of psychological and psychiatric problems. As with all the other types of mental health problems in fathers, it is important to remember that a large number of children of alcoholic fathers grow up to be well-adjusted adults.

DEPRESSION

Unlike the topic of alcohol abuse in fathers, the topic of depression in fathers is relatively little researched. A number of psychologists have noted that a great many studies have been conducted to examine the connection between depression in mothers and problems in their children but relatively little work has explored depression in fathers. This pattern of research may result partly from the prevalence of depression in adults. Women, and therefore mothers, are about twice as likely as men, and therefore fathers, to experience severe depression. Major depressive disorder is experienced by 5% to 12% of men and 10% to 25% of women at some point in their lives. Although most people experience periods of feeling sad and refer to themselves as feeling depressed at times, major depressive disorder is characterized by at least two weeks of extreme sadness, loss of interest in nearly all activities that used to be enjoyable, feelings of extreme edginess, changes in appetite, changes in sleeping patterns, feelings of worthlessness, and even a desire to be dead. The type of depression that is discussed here is sometimes referred to as unipolar depression, which differs from bipolar or manic depression (not reviewed here). Although there are few studies of fathers who have experienced unipolar depression, there are enough studies to lead us to relatively firm conclusions.[12]

In general, children of fathers who are depressed show more mental health problems than children of fathers who are psychologically healthy. When children of depressed fathers are compared with children of depressed mothers, few differences are found. In other words, whether the depressed parent is the father or the mother, children seem to be at similar risk for developing mental health problems.[13]

Many people are surprised to learn that fathers, like mothers, can also experience postpartum depression after the birth of a child. For fathers and mothers alike, parents' depressive feelings before the birth of the child seem to be related to the level of depressive feelings after the birth of the child. Like mothers' postpartum depression, fathers' postpartum depression is related to problems in children even years after the initial depression.[14]

Mental health problems experienced by children with a depressed parent vary depending on a variety of factors, including the family environment. When there is a lot of fighting and arguing between parents in a family with a depressed parent, children are more likely to develop problems that are externalizing in nature (e.g., oppositional behavior and conduct problems). When there are relatively low levels of fighting and arguing between parents in a family with a depressed parent, children are more likely to develop problems that are internalizing in nature (e.g., depression and anxiety).[15]

Evidence suggests that when one parent is depressed, the other parent's behavior can significantly influence the well-being of the child. When a child has a mother who is depressed but has a father who is psychologically healthy, that child will be less likely to develop problems than other children with a depressed mother. For teenagers, a good father-teenager relationship can protect the teen from the possible adverse effects of having a depressed mother. Luckily, fathers often change their behavior to accommodate changes in the family that result when a mother is depressed. Based on direct observations of families, husbands of depressed women showed more nurturant and caring behavior toward their children than did husbands without a depressed wife.[16]

Overall, it appears that depression in either a father or a mother is related to significant mental health problems in children. There seems to be similar risk for the development of problems, regardless of whether it is the father or the mother who is depressed.

ANXIETY DISORDERS

A number of different anxiety disorders are evident in adulthood; these include panic disorder with or without agoraphobia, specific phobias, social phobias, obsessive-compulsive disorder, generalized anxiety disorder, and post traumatic stress disorder. Anxiety disorders are relatively common in relation to other types of problems in mental health. For example, approximately 2.5% of adults experience panic disorder at some point in their lives, and approximately 10.5% of adults are diagnosed with a specific phobia at some point in their lives. As with research on children diagnosed with an anxiety disorder, extremely few studies have investigated the children of fathers diagnosed with an anxiety disorder, and most of those studies explored children of fathers who had combat-related post traumatic stress disorder.

Ironically, the one main study that explored an anxiety disorder other than post traumatic stress was able to evaluate only children of fathers diagnosed with both an anxiety disorder and depression. These children were found to show higher levels of mental health problems than children of psychologically healthy fathers, but there were no separate analyses for different types of anxiety disorders that the fathers had experienced.[17]

Although not in a formal diagnostic category, many parents experience anxiety when separated from their children because the youngsters are at day care or at school. Most studies that have explored this type of anxiety have explored only mothers' feelings of anxiety, but one well-designed study also explored fathers' feelings of anxiety upon leaving their young children at a center-based child care facility. Results showed that fathers experience about the same amount of anxiety as mothers when leaving their children (aged 1 to 5) at a day care center. This study highlighted the importance of exploring parenting experiences that might be similar for fathers and mothers.[18]

Three studies have evaluated children of fathers diagnosed with post traumatic stress disorder resulting from combat experiences in either World War II or the Vietnam War. Results of these studies showed that young children and adult children of veterans who experienced the disorder were more maladjusted than young children and adult children of veterans who had not experienced post traumatic stress.[19]

Overall, surprisingly little research has been done on children of fathers with an anxiety disorder. A number of researchers have explored anxiety disorders in mothers and have also included a few fathers in the studies, but results have yet to be reported for mothers and fathers separately. Given the relatively large number of adults who experience some type of post traumatic stress disorder, this is an area that needs immediate attention from family researchers.[20]

SCHIZOPHRENIA

Of all of the mental health problems discussed in this book, schizophrenia is probably the most severe and the most debilitating both for the individual experiencing the problem and for the individual's family members and friends who try to provide adequate care. As noted in Chapter 4, schizophrenia is diagnosed when an individual is out of touch with reality and cannot care for him or herself for a period of at least six months. The most notable signs of schizophrenia are when an individual hears voices or sees things that are not really there (characteristics that are known as hallucinations) or when an individual believes things that are clearly not true (characteristics that are known as delusions). Individuals diagnosed with schizophrenia often communicate in an unusual manner, such as having incoherent speech. Because of these symptoms, another characteristic of schizophrenia is that the individual has limitations in his or her occupational, social, and interpersonal functioning. Although devastating, schizophrenia is a relatively rare disorder. Less than 1% of adults are diagnosed with schizophrenia throughout their lifetime.

Unfortunately, extremely little is known about the offspring of fathers diagnosed with schizophrenia. This lack of research is attributable not only to the rarity of the disorder but also to the process by which many of these men father children. Men who are diagnosed with schizophrenia are unlikely to marry or to take part in parenting their children. In one study of fathers diagnosed with schizophrenia and receiving medication and therapy through an outpatient mental health center, 30% of the fathers were raising the children along with the children's mother, 60% reported that the mother was raising the children by herself, and 10% did not know the whereabouts of their children. Unfortunately, there is a pattern known as *assortative mating*, which reflects the likelihood that men or women with psychiatric problems tend to pair up and have children with partners who are also experiencing psychiatric problems. Thus, for those fathers who did not take part in rearing their own children, it is likely that the mothers were also experiencing a psychiatric problem that may have negatively influenced the child's family environment. As noted in Chapter 4, there is a relatively high genetic loading with schizophrenia, but environmental factors also influence which children will likely go on to develop schizophrenia themselves and which will not.[21]

Some studies have followed children who have a parent diagnosed with schizophrenia, but most of these studies have combined children who have a schizophrenic father with children who have a schizophrenic mother. Results from these studies suggest that children with a parent diagnosed with schizophrenia are at increased risk for the development of a number of different mental health problems. In addition, children of schizophrenic fathers are as much at risk for the development of problems as children of schizophrenic mothers. These conclusions, however, are tentative given the dearth of research on fathers diagnosed with schizophrenia.[22]

Overall, extremely little is known about fathers diagnosed with schizophrenia. Because of the severity of this disorder, it would be helpful for more explorations of what it is like for children who have a father experiencing schizophrenia, regardless of whether or not the children know their father.

PHYSICAL ABUSE

Although no formal diagnostic category exists for adults who physically abuse their children, there is a great deal of research on parents who physically abuse their children and on the impact of this abuse. Even though mothers and fathers are about equally as likely to physically abuse their children, the majority of research in this area nonetheless focuses on mothers. Ironically, some research even explores mothers' behavior with children who were physically abused by someone else (e.g., the father or another caretaker). One example of a well-designed study compared fathers and mothers of children who had been abused but also looked at which parent perpetrated the abuse. Results of the study suggested that gender of the parent was not important on a number of abuse and stress measures; instead, whether or not the parent was the perpetrator of the abuse was the most important parental characteristic.[23]

Physical abuse can lead to serious physical, behavioral, and emotional problems in children. Sadly, it is estimated that 30% of abused children go on to abuse their own children. It is important to realize, however, that approximately 70% of abused children apparently do not go on to abuse their own children.[24]

When mothers and fathers who physically abuse their children are compared, a number of differences are found. Fathers tend to commit physical abuse more severely violent in nature (e.g., using or threatening to use a gun or a knife, scalding or burning the child, biting the child, kicking the child, hitting the child with a fist or with an object). Mothers tend to commit abuse associated with less severe forms of violence (e.g., pushing, grabbing, slapping, shoving, or spanking the child). As you might imagine, both types of abuse are harmful to children.[25]

Not surprisingly, fathers and mothers of physically abused children show greater current mental health problems and they report more mental health problems in their past when compared with fathers and mothers who do not physically abuse their children. Fathers who physically abuse their children are often violent with their children when they are drinking alcohol in excessive quantities.[26]

Interestingly, even when children are not abused themselves but they witness abuse of their parent, they experience emotional problems. A number of studies have shown that when a father or a father figure abuses a child's mother, the children suffer emotional problems (such as depression) to the same degree that they would have shown had they been abused themselves. These studies show that violence within the family is harmful no matter who is the target of the physical abuse.[27]

SEXUAL ABUSE

Sexual abuse of children can also be devastating. Although many people think of a stranger in a secluded park as the most likely child molester, the overwhelming majority of child sexual abuse perpetrators are known by the child and most often are from within the family. In the case of sexual abuse by a family member, the overwhelming majority of child sexual abuse is perpetrated by fathers or father figures such as a stepfather or a boyfriend of the child's mother. Sadly, children who are sexually abused by their father or by a father figure experience significantly more emotional problems than do children who are molested by someone other than a father or father figure. One study found that over half the children who were sexually abused by their father went on to experience post traumatic stress disorder in which they had nightmares and flashbacks about the abuse, experienced strong feelings of sadness or anxiety after the abuse, and experienced declines in their schoolwork or social relationships as a result of the abuse. When compared with girls who were not sexually abused, girls who were abused by their father were more likely to experience mental health problems, to try to run away or kill themselves during their teen years, or to become pregnant as a teenager. It is also important to acknowledge that boys are at risk for sexual abuse and exhibit problems similar to those girls experience as a result of sexual abuse.[28]

Many children blame themselves for the sexual abuse, often because the perpetrator has told them they are to blame. Professionals consistently argue, however, that the perpetrator—not the child and not the mother—is responsible for the sexual abuse. Unfortunately, some misguided professionals have focused on blaming mothers for allowing their child to be sexually abused. Yet again mothers are often incorrectly blamed for fathers' behavior. When mothers of sexually abused children were compared based on who abused their child (the father, another relative, or a nonrelative), the only difference that emerged was that the mothers whose child was sexually abused by the father were also more likely to have experienced physical abuse by the child's father. As discussed in Chapter 3, it is important not to blame mothers for events that are out of their control. Such blame can compound the negative effects of child sexual abuse and should be addressed therapeutically if it is relevant to the child or to the adult survivor of sexual abuse.[29]

When considering what differentiates fathers who sexually abuse their children and those who do not, one study of sexually abused daughters found intriguing results. Sexually abusive fathers were more likely to have been mistreated by their parents during their own childhood; these fathers were also more likely to have been either partially or fully absent during the first three years of their daughter's life. It may be that a father's presence and involvement in the early stages of childrearing, when the infant is completely dependent on its parents, may help the father to solidify his role as a father and thus make him less likely to eventually perceive his daughter as an outlet for sexual aggression. Conversely, it could be that fathers who were stable enough to be involved in early parenting duties were the fathers who were stable enough not to sexually abuse their daughters.[30]

Given the potential devastating effects of child sexual abuse, it is important to seek ways to prevent such abuse from ever occurring. Many school systems now have prevention programs aimed at teaching children the differences between "good touch" and "bad touch" or at teaching them to tell someone if they are being sexually abused. Unfortunately, many of these programs focus only on sexual abuse by strangers and fail to address the possibility that the abuse is perpetrated by someone the child loves (such as a father or another relative). A number of professionals have argued that in addition to promoting these types of training programs, we also need to target potential perpetrators in order to prevent the abuse from occurring in the first place. The larger issue of sexual victimization of children, with the concomitant abuse of power and control over children, could be addressed by teaching from an early age about more healthy sexuality. One theory about why men sexually abuse their children is that from early on, boys are taught that emotional closeness is tied directly to sexuality. It may be that for some men, the warm emotions they feel toward their child are misinterpreted as sexual feelings because they have not been able to differentiate between sexual feelings and feelings of love and concern. Obviously, these sociocultural issues are difficult to tackle and will not be easily remedied. However, given the prevalence of child sexual abuse and given the often devastating effects of child sexual abuse, greater attention must be paid to preventing the occurence of such abuse.[31]

SUMMARY

Overall, children are at risk for developing mental health problems when their father experiences mental health problems and when their father is physically or sexually abusive. Although there is rarely a direct one-to-one connection between fathers' and children's mental health problems, children of disturbed fathers experience a great many more problems than do children of fathers who are psychologically healthy. This pattern seems to be true regardless of the problem the father experiences. In other words, whether the father is depressed or alcoholic or anxiety disordered, children are at risk for the development of mental health problems. This pattern also appears consistent whether it is the father or the mother who is experiencing mental health problems. When faced with either a father or a mother with mental health problems, children seem to be at equal risk for the development of their own problems. Luckily, if the other parent is well functioning or if there are other protective factors in the child, the family, or the community, children of disordered parents need not be destined to develop emotional and behavioral problems.

6

WHAT TO DO WHEN THERE ARE MENTAL HEALTH PROBLEMS IN FATHERS OR CHILDREN

•

Having choked, you are able to chew;
having fallen, you are able to walk.

—PROVERB OF AFRICA

Now that you know a bit more about the connections between mental health problems in fathers and their children, let's consider how these mental health problems can be treated. First, the effectiveness of therapy and different issues related to therapy with children and fathers are discussed, and then specific tips for how to find help are given.

DOES THERAPY WORK?

The effectiveness of therapy has been studied ever since the use of therapy began. The simple answer to the question, "Does therapy work?" is "Yes, usually." But given that it is not a simple question, I won't leave you with a simple answer.

One way of determining whether or not therapy works is to ask clients who have been in therapy. In 1995 a large survey was done by *Consumer Reports* in which adults who had been in therapy were asked if they were satisfied with the therapy. An overwhelming majority (close to 90%) said that they had been helped by the therapy they had received. Based on clients' self-reports, clients who were in therapy for over six months reported more improvement in their psychological symptoms than did clients who were in therapy for a shorter period of time. There were no differences in clients' satisfaction with therapy based on whether the client saw a psychologist, psychiatrist, or social worker. Overall, the *Consumer Reports* survey suggested that therapy usually works to alleviate the problems about which clients seek help.[1]

Although the *Consumer Reports* survey was a powerful comment on the effectiveness of therapy, there is also a need to evaluate the effectiveness of therapy in a more formal, scientific manner. A more formal way of evaluating whether therapy works is to conduct controlled studies that allow the researcher to look carefully at how the therapy was conducted and what type of good and bad effects emerged for the client after therapy. If you harken back to the research methods discussion at the beginning of Chapter 4, you will recall that researchers cannot claim that one thing "causes" another thing unless they use an experimental research design. In the case of looking at the effectiveness of therapy, an experimental research design would consist of the researcher randomly assigning clients in the study to one of many different therapies or even to a "waiting list" control group. Two primary research designs are used to study the effectiveness of therapy: comparing the effectiveness of two different types of treatment (e.g., seeing if clients in the behavior therapy group were better or worse off than clients in the cognitive therapy group after a set amount of time) and comparing one type of therapy with no therapy (e.g., seeing if clients who received client-centered therapy were better or worse off than clients who were put on a waiting list to delay treatment for a period of time). The most sophisticated research design is to combine these two types of studies and to compare two types of therapies with a waiting list control group. When clients are put on a waiting list to delay treatment, they are most often provided with treatment at the end of the study. There are, of course, ethical concerns about intentionally putting a distressed person on a waiting list for research purposes, but the greater concern is that just comparing the effectiveness of two types of therapies does not enable the researcher to determine if the passage of time (as with the no-therapy control group) is by itself also beneficial.

Before going on to discuss the results of these types of studies, I should make it clear that researchers must have clients' written permission before the client is involved in a research study. There are federal, state, and local guidelines researchers must follow, and for most studies these days, researchers must have the clients' written permission before placing them in a research study. This written permission is referred to as "informed consent," which means that potential research participants must be informed about the study and they must provide their consent to be in the study. The "informed" portion of informed consent requires that the potential participant be told about the purpose of the study, any possible harmful effects of the study, how the information from the study will be used, that the information is confidential or even anonymous in some cases, how the results of the study will be helpful to the participant or to the larger community, and whom to contact should there be any problems with involvement in the study. The "consent" portion of informed consent requires participants to provide their voluntary permission to be involved in the study, which means that they should not be forced or coerced into a study, that they should not be penalized in any way if they do not participate in the study, and that they can withdraw from the study at any point without negative ramifications. For children under 18 years of age, parents must provide their written consent; depending on the age of the child, most researchers also ask for the child's written assent to take part in the study.

Whether the study is involved with the effectiveness of therapy or some other topic, researchers must first have the research approved by an institutional review board (IRB) before the research study can be conducted. Research universities all have an IRB that follows federal, state, and local guidelines for the completion of research on humans. Comparable guidelines must be followed when using animals in research. Most departments of psychology have a departmental research review committee as well as the university IRB. These review committees have been put into place to provide safeguards in the research process and to protect the rights of potential research participants. We have all heard about egregious violations of human rights in the name of "science," and these review boards were instituted as a response to these violations of human rights. You might still come across an example of unethical research being conducted these days, but current guidelines are meant to protect the public as much as possible.

With some reassurance about the research process, let's get back to considering the effectiveness of therapy. Once individual studies of therapy effectiveness, called outcome studies, are completed, other researchers can combine the results of these studies to get an overall view of the effectiveness of different types of therapies. The process of

combining the overall results of these outcome studies is known as
meta-analysis. Meta-analytic studies allow researchers to make conclusions that are much stronger than the conclusions from any individual outcome study. A number of meta-analyses have explored the
effectiveness of therapy, some having explored child therapy, others
family therapy.

In general, meta-analytic studies of therapy with children suggest
that any therapy is better than no therapy. To argue that any one type
of therapy is better than another type of therapy is less clear-cut.
There is some indication that behavioral therapies (e.g., therapies that
work to change the problem behavior directly) are more effective than
nonbehavioral therapies (e.g., therapies that do not address the problem behavior directly but, rather, have the child talk about his or her
problems or family). Because this conclusion is not consistently found
in meta-analyses, it remains to be seen if one type of therapy is supe-
rior to other types of therapy. The same can be said for studies of family therapy. A meta-analysis of family therapy suggested that family
therapy was better than no therapy, but that it was not consistently
better than therapy that only involved the child.[2]

Certain types of problems are more effectively treated by certain
types of treatments. For example, certain anxiety disorders, such as
panic disorder or specific phobias, are best treated with cognitive-
behavioral therapy. Medication is often the treatment of choice for
AD/HD. Between 73% and 77% of children diagnosed with AD/HD receive substantial benefits from psychostimulant medication such as
Ritalin. In addition to the consideration of medication for AD/HD, behavioral and cognitive-behavioral techniques can also help children
and their families deal with high levels of activity and inattention. As
suggested later in the chapter, professionals need to be sought out in
order to determine what treatment is most appropriate for that individual child and family. These studies have been summarized for therapy effectiveness in general, without attention to mothers' and
fathers' involvement in the therapy. The next logical topic to consider
is whether mothers' involvement or fathers' involvement is more
beneficial for effective therapy.[3]

DOES THERAPY WORK BETTER WHEN FATHERS
ARE INVOLVED?

Although not very much research has explored this question, the
tentative answer to the question, "Does therapy work better when fa-

thers are involved?" is "No, not necessarily." However, the more complicated answer is that for certain therapies, it is not important which parent is involved—it is important only that one of the parents be involved. In other words, whether the mother or the father takes part in the therapy does not matter as long as one of the parents or other primary caretakers is involved. Most research on this topic has dealt with behavioral parent training, which is a form of therapy that helps parents learn behavior management skills for their children. The techniques that are taught are straightforward; they include the need to spend "quality" time with your child when there is no set agenda for having to accomplish something, the need to pay attention to your child's good behavior, the importance of having consistent and known consequences (such as time out or loss of a privilege) to bad behavior, and the necessity of having consistency in responses to good and bad behavior across times (e.g., whether it is 6:30 P.M. and the parent has had a bad day at work or whether it is at 11:00 A.M. on a bright, sunny Saturday morning when the parent is in a good mood) and across places (e.g., at the mother's home, at the father's home, at the grandparents' home, at school, at day care, or at the grocery store in the cookie aisle). Note that these are goals therapists try to help families work in to their own daily routines. In general, behavioral parent training has been found to be very effective in decreasing the bad behavior and increasing the good behavior of young children. The treatment is most effective for children aged 2 to 11 who show externalizing behavior problems such as not following directions, being oppositional, throwing tantrums, fighting, and arguing.[4]

Some researchers have explored whether it is more effective to have mothers only, fathers only, or both mothers and fathers involved in this type of treatment. In general, no difference is evident in the behavioral improvements of children whose mother only, father only, or mother and father both participated in the treatment. This lack of difference may be the result of what is called "unprogrammed learning," where the parent involved in therapy communicates what he or she has learned in therapy to the other parent or caretakers in the child's life. Unprogrammed learning is considered a benefit of a parent's involvement in behavioral parent training, given that other caretakers in the child's life should be involved in helping to provide consistent consequences to the child's behavior. When both parents are involved in behavioral parent training, both mothers and fathers tend to show similar levels of improvement in their parenting skills.[5]

For other types of therapy, the question remains as to what type of improvements might occur for mothers and fathers when both parents are involved in therapy. Most studies in this area have found that mothers and fathers benefit equally from involvement in therapy and that there are rarely any differences in the improvements made by mothers and fathers. For example, both mothers and fathers were able to decrease their use of coercive and aggressive behavior with their children when a family systems and focused casework approach was used. One study did find that ecological family therapy with delinquent boys lead to more improvements in the mother-teenager relationship than in the father-teenager relationship, but most studies have found that mothers and fathers show similar improvements when involved in therapy with their children.[6]

One study highlighted the importance of including both mothers and fathers in child-oriented treatment because doing so allows the therapist to address any conflicts between the parents that need to be addressed. In a behavioral parent-training program for the parents of toddlers who showed oppositional behavior, parents were taught to work together cooperatively, to solve problems together, and to stop arguing, which made the behavioral parent training even more effective. This study pointed out the importance of not only addressing a child's problems but also of trying to help parents decrease their own fighting—regardless of whether or not the parents are married to each other.[7]

Overall, there is not overwhelming evidence that including fathers in therapy with children is any better than including mothers in therapy unless issues between the parents need to be addressed. Given the strong connection between parents' conflict with each other and the development of emotional and behavioral problems in children, it is crucial that problematic parent relationships be addressed in therapy intended to help children.[8]

GETTING FATHERS INVOLVED IN THERAPY

A number of researchers and clinicians have written about the strong hesitation many fathers feel about becoming involved in therapy for their children. Professionals may either overtly or covertly encourage fathers not to participate in therapy by not suggesting that their attendance is important for therapy. Many clinical researchers have not included fathers in the therapy being studied, and many clinicians fail to include fathers in therapy oriented toward helping the child. Much has been written on why fathers might not want to get involved in therapy for their children, including that men are less likely than women to get involved in therapy for themselves, that mothers are often given the responsibility of taking children to doctors' and therapists' appointments, and that fathers may be reluctant to get involved in therapy because they fear being found lacking as a parent. Fathers who do not live with their children should also be considered for inclusion in the child's therapy, especially if the child or mother has had difficulty dealing with the parental separation or divorce.[9]

Fathers are more likely to become involved in family therapy if they have received therapy in the past, if they are nontraditional in their gender role orientation, and if they perceive their family problems to be very serious. Fathers are also more likely to be involved in family therapy if the therapist explains that father involvement in therapy is necessary and if the mental health clinic offers evening and weekend appointments.[10]

It may not just be fathers' hesitation that prevents their participation in therapy for their child and family. It may be that therapists' own issues are influencing whether or not fathers are asked to be involved in therapy. One study compared therapists who did or did not routinely ask for father involvement in therapy and found that therapists were more likely to include fathers in therapy if the therapist was male, was newer to the profession, was educated in family therapy techniques (as opposed to being trained only in child therapy techniques), and was egalitarian in his or her beliefs about family responsibilities needing to be equal. Thus, therapists as well as fathers and mothers themselves should consider why a particular father has not been involved in a therapeutic situation that might benefit from the father's participation.[11]

Therapists committed to getting fathers involved in therapy can use a number of techniques to engage fathers in the therapeutic process. Given that mothers are often the person to make the first call to set up the therapy appointment, therapists can through them ask to speak to the father directly in order to clarify that all family members, including the father himself, are expected to be involved in therapy. The therapist can also point out the importance of getting every family member's perspective on the problems that need to be addressed in therapy. If the father appears hesitant about involving himself in therapy, the therapist can acknowledge that many fathers are initially hesitant but that once they begin the process, they often find therapy useful. If the father uses a busy work schedule as an excuse for not wanting to attend therapy, therapists can gently challenge the father's priorities and question him on the importance of helping his child with the presenting problems. If a father or mother is still so angry at the other parent that both parents refuse to be in the same room together, the therapist can arrange separate appointments to discuss the therapeutic needs of the child with each parent separately. In this case, however, a therapeutic goal might be to help the parents communicate directly if they are to continue to co-parent the child and not place the child between them in their arguments.[12]

Once therapy begins, many special needs should be considered when involving fathers in the treatment. Teen fathers are often ignored when their children are involved in therapy, but surveys suggest that many teen fathers want to be more involved in their children's lives. Fathers of all ages who do not have custody of their children have special needs and concerns when it comes to their own mental health and the mental health of their children. Therapists of noncustodial fathers may need to deal with many of the following issues: children's rejection of the noncustodial father; fathers' rejections of their children; difficulties with holiday and birthday arrangements; the children's feelings of being emotionally caught between the mother, the father, and any stepparents; and concerns about the paternal grandparents' role with the children. Fathers who are the primary caretaker of the children also have special needs to be addressed by therapists. Because single fatherhood is much less common than single motherhood, single fathers may feel isolated in their parenting role. Similar to single mothers, single fathers are often overwhelmed by the responsibilities of raising a child by themselves; they may be concerned about their own adequacy as a parent, and they may need help finding a balance between time and energy for parenting in relation to getting on with their own personal adjustment. Therapists must also be able to deal with fathers' and families' particular needs surrounding ethnic and cultural values and sexual orientation.[13]

Regardless of the special needs of the family seeking therapy, the bottom line is that therapy is more effective than no therapy. If families are concerned about a family member, they should do something about the problem before it gets worse.

HOW TO FIND HELP

What can families do when their children, fathers, or mothers experience mental health problems? Based on what you've just read, the most obvious answer is that they seek professional help with a mental health professional. In addition to the suggestions that follow, interested readers may want to go to the library to find the *Consumer Reports* article that discussed the survey on the helpfulness of therapy. The article not only reviews the survey results, but also suggests similarities and differences between types of mental health professionals, identifies types of therapies most appropriate for specific problems, and explains how to find a therapist that fits your needs.[14]

As for finding help, many health insurance companies cover mental health services for individuals, couples, and families. The type of mental health professional you seek can have an impact on the services available. For example, only someone with a medical degree can prescribe medication; so if you are seeking medication, you should discuss the issues of concern with your family doctor or you should seek out a psychiatrist, who has been trained in prescribing medication for mental health problems. Other mental health professionals, such as psychologists, mental health counselors, marriage and family counselors, and social workers, cannot prescribe medication but they often work in conjunction with a psychiatrist who can prescribe medication. Most mental health professionals, including psychiatrists, psychologists, mental health counselors, marriage and family counselors, and social workers, can conduct therapy or counseling when it is needed.

Individuals in need of help should consult their insurance company to see if therapy and psychiatric coverage for medications are covered and to find out to what extent these services are covered. For example, some insurance plans have a list of "preferred providers" from which you must choose a therapist. For those people covered by public assistance such as medicare or medicaid, mental health services are often covered, but the coverage needs to be verified with the appropriate agency. Be forewarned that in the private sector as well as in the public sector, a number of health maintenance organizations (HMOs) put a limit on how many therapy sessions will be covered.

Before proceeding with therapy, it is in your best interest to see what is and what is not covered by your insurance company. If you do not have health insurance or if your health insurance does not cover mental health issues, then you should locate the community mental health center in your area. Community mental health centers have been developed throughout the United States to provide mental health services, including both therapy and medication, at a very low or no fee at all. Low-fee, high-quality services are also often available through an outpatient clinic at a local university. Many departments of psychology, psychiatry, counseling, and social work have mental health clinics that are open to the public. A few calls to your local college or university might help you identify options for affordable services.

Note that regardless of how services are accessed, most professionals conduct some type of testing, otherwise known as assessment, in order to determine if therapy is needed and if so, what type of therapy might be the most effective. Some professionals conduct very formal testing, which often consists of structured tests and questionnaires that can take many hours for children and families to complete. Other professionals conduct a less formal assessment procedure, usually by interviewing the relevant individuals (e.g., the child, the mother, and the father). In either case, feel free to ask professionals about their assessment procedures, to ask about their therapeutic orientation (e.g., to ask if they are they more Freudian or behavioral in their techniques), and to ask about the plans for therapy. Sometimes children are seen alone in therapy with a consultation between the parents and the therapist, sometimes parents are seen in therapy without the children, sometimes the entire family is seen in therapy, and sometimes family members are invited to join therapy that is conducted in groups. These options can be discussed during the first contact with the mental health professional.

For children with problems, mental health services can also be accessed through the public school system in most communities. This process may be complicated, given that testing must document that there are problems that interfere with the child's functioning in school. Interested parents are encouraged to discuss the feasibility and appropriateness of mental health services for their child with a school psychologist or a guidance counselor. Ironically, these services are often more easily accessible if the child attends a public school rather than a private school. Federal law mandates that special services for children who are learning disabled, emotionally troubled, developmentally delayed, or physically challenged be provided through the public school system. Private schools hold no such federal mandate, so sometimes parents must choose to have their child attend a public school in order to receive special services that may not be available in private schools.

In addition to seeking help through their insurance company or through a local community mental health center, adults with problems may turn to their places of employment, many of which have some type of mental health services available on site. These programs, often called Employee Assistance Programs (EAPs), offer mental health counseling and may also provide educational classes meant to help prevent problems from occurring; topics of these classes, include parenting skills, anger management, and social skills enrichment. The programs are often available only at larger companies and organizations; employees must consult with their personnel or benefits' office to find out if they have an EAP through the workplace.

In addition to these formal settings for professional help, there are also other resources for individuals and families experiencing problems. Many churches have pastoral counseling available for members. Support groups through community organizations can also be helpful for individuals. Local meetings are held by nationally organized groups such as Parents without Partners, CHAD (for parents with children diagnosed with AD/HD), Alliance for the Mentally Ill (a support group for parents and family members of individuals with mental health problems), and the Depressive and Manic Depressive Association (a support group for people who have experienced depression or manic depression and for their families and loved ones). Most communities also have a variety of support groups that have developed out of specialized needs in that community. The best way to find out about these support groups is to call your local community mental health center or to look in your local paper for announcements about meetings in your area. Organizations with national headquarters are listed in the back of this book with addresses and phone numbers.

For families where violence is an issue, most communities have some type of "safe house" where mothers and children can be safe from an abusive father or father figure. These agencies often have support groups for fathers who have problems with anger control and for the mothers and children who are at risk for violence. If the violence is solely directed at the child (by the mother, father, or other caretaker), every state has a system for responding to and for trying to prevent the occurrence of physical and sexual abuse against children. Each state calls the agency something different, but usually these agencies are referred to as the child protective agency for the state. Ordinary citizens (such as a concerned neighbor or a concerned family friend) are allowed to report their concerns to this state agency. It is important to note that teachers, day care workers, psychologists, doctors and other professionals involved with children are mandated to report their suspicions of child abuse and neglect to this governmental agency. In other words, these professionals have to report their suspicions of physical, sexual, and emotional abuse or neglect, even if the parents promise to stop abusing their child. Such mandated reporting is meant to ensure that the child abuse is stopped. You can check with Information in your area or with your local police or sheriff's department to find out how to report your suspicions of abuse.

As for other resources specific to fathers, you may want to explore a national organization called the National Fatherhood Initiative (see the organization listing at the back of the book for how to contact this organization). Although this organization does not provide direct mental health services or support groups, it can provide fathers with resources about fathering, especially with regard to custody and co-parenting issues. Their primary focus is the restoration of responsible fatherhood in America. There is also a network of professionals, called the National Center on Fathers and Families, dedicated to using research and social policy to improve the lives of children, fathers, and mothers.

Whether you are an individual adult experiencing problems in your own life or in your romantic relationship, a parent experiencing problems with the stressfulness of parenting, a parent whose child is experiencing problems, or a co-parent experiencing problems with the child's other parent, I encourage you to seek help from someone. At a minimum, try to talk to other people you know; you may find that many of them are experiencing or have experienced similar problems. Friends and co-workers may be able to give other suggestions for helpful resources within your community.

Many parents, especially single parents, feel isolated because of the demands of their job and their family responsibilities. They may be relieved to discover that other parents feel just as overwhelmed. Often, sharing these feelings with others can help a stressed parent come up with ideas to make the situation a little more tolerable. For example, I knew of two single parents who were overwhelmed with the responsibilities of taking care of their children, working a full-time job outside of the home, and having no extra money to hire a babysitter so they might get a little rest and relaxation away from the home. These two parents decided to swap childcare duties each weekend so that one would take care of the children for four hours on a Saturday while the other parent ran errands and went out with friends. The next weekend the roles were swapped so that the first parent could have four hours of rest and relaxation. Although it can take time to develop such creative solutions, they can be helpful for parents whose resources are stretched to the limits.

For parents who have a child with special needs, whether needs are related to physical, developmental, or emotional challenges, often respite services are available at a low-fee or at no fee, so the child can have high-quality care while the parent is allowed a break from parenting duties. Different communities have different availabilities of these services, but a few phone calls might lead you to find a much needed break. In some communities, you might even find respite care where you least expect it. For example, in Tampa, the United Cerebral Palsy Organization offers respite care for parents of children with not only CP, but also for parents of children with other developmental or psychological disorders. Your local community mental health agency or a service organization such as the United Way might be able to help you find these types of respite services.

The most important thing to realize is that a difficult situation can always be changed for the better. Sometimes it takes a lot of frustrating phone calls to find out where to get affordable help, but it is important to try to deal with problems of concern to you and your family. For parents of troubled children, finding a good therapist for your child can be perhaps the most long-lasting gift that you ever give to your child. If you are able to deal with problems in your child's early years, you and your child may be saved from experiencing more severe problems in later years. For extremely stressed or troubled parents, getting help for yourself can often be the best way to help your child. Given the connection between mental health problems in parents and problems in children, parents should not feel selfish in seeking help for themselves. Such help will probably help the entire family in the long run.

FEELING SAFE IN THERAPY

Since I discussed the ethics of conducting research, let me also discuss the ethics of conducting therapy, given that some people may be hesitant about seeking therapy because they have heard about unscrupulous therapists through talk shows, in the newspaper or as depicted in the latest movie. It is a personal pet peeve of mine that therapists are often portrayed in the media as unethical, which is not reflective of the majority of therapists. There is no question that sometimes a therapist does something really wrong, such as becoming romantically involved with a client or sharing information that should have been confidential. The general public often responds to these cases with legitimate anger. Like the public, most professionals respond to these documented cases of unethical behavior with outrage.

That a few unscrupulous individuals can besmirch the reputation of an entire profession makes me furious. On average, mental health professionals are ethical and maintain the client-therapist relationship with the highest integrity. But still, the images that we see in movies (such as *The Evening Star, Mr. Jones, Final Analysis, The Prince of Tides,* and *The First Wives' Club*) and on television (one of the sisters on the television show *Sisters* and Fraiser and Diane on the television show *Cheers*) is of therapists sleeping with their clients or with family members of their clients. These examples are in direct violation of ethical guidelines.

Therapists cannot have what are called multiple relationships with their clients. That is, therapists cannot serve in two roles with their clients (e.g., they cannot have someone as a client who is also their student, they cannot have someone as a client who is also their business partner, and they cannot have someone as a client who is also their romantic partner). Often, clients have sexual feelings toward their therapist, but these feelings are rarely only about sex. Therapists should not act on propositions from their clients no matter how much they want to convince themselves that it is okay. In studies of clients who have become sexually involved with their therapists, almost always some psychological harm is done to the client. In anonymous studies of therapists willing to acknowledge having been sexually involved with a client, the small percentage of therapists so involved reported having relationships with a number of clients. In other words, a small handful of therapists are unethical and they take advantage of a number of clients. This pattern alone suggests that the therapists are becoming sexually involved with their clients to fulfill their own needs rather than any needs of an individual client.[15]

Why is it so important that therapists not engage in multiple relationships with their clients? The reason has to do with the special nature of a therapeutic relationship. The therapeutic relationship is almost sacred in the way that a client reveals his or her innermost concerns and feelings to a therapist, who in return discloses almost nothing about him or herself. Therapists do not usually self-disclose because the focus should be on the client's needs and best interests rather than on the therapist's own issues. Therapists can deal with their own issues by going into therapy themselves. Given that clients share so much personal information about themselves, they are vulnerable in relation to the therapist should the relationship change to anything other than a therapist-client relationship. There are therefore a great many ethical and legal guidelines protecting the therapist-client relationship.

In addition to the guidelines set to protect the therapeutic relationship there are also strict guidelines to control the confidentiality of what is said in therapy. Based on professional ethics guidelines and state laws, information shared in a therapeutic relationship is completely confidential and cannot be shared outside that relationship except in rare cases (such as in response to a court order or when the client gives his or her written permission for the therapist to share the information). There are, however, important limits to confidentiality that are set by state law, but these limits are consistent throughout the United States and many other countries. Four basic limits to confidentiality are followed in nearly every mental health profession in nearly every state in the Union: Danger to self, danger to another, physical abuse or neglect of a child or incapacitated person or elderly person, and sexual abuse of a child. If any one of these dangers or abuses is strongly suspected, then the therapist has to do something to try to prevent it from occurring.

In the case of possible danger to self, a therapist must try to determine the imminence or likelihood of suicide. In other words, the therapist must try to figure out if the client will act on his or her suicidal wishes. If suicide is considered imminent, then the therapist must do something to try to prevent the suicide. In many cases, the therapist can help the client to gain admission into a psychiatric hospital on a voluntary basis. If the client is unwilling to seek protection from him or herself voluntarily and the therapist determines the suicide to be imminent, then the therapist is mandated to break confidentiality and to get other mental health professionals and legal professionals involved to hospitalize the client involuntarily in order to prevent the suicide and in order to help the client become less suicidal. It should be noted that many people, whether or not in therapy, have suicidal thoughts and wishes at some point in their lives. Therapists are trained to try to determine which clients can work on these suicidal issues through the normal therapeutic process and which clients need more intensified services in order to prevent the suicide.

In the case of possible danger to another—if a therapist thinks that a client is about to kill someone, for example—the therapist must do something to try to prevent the murder from occurring. This prevention may be in the form of contacting the police, or it may be in the form of trying to have the client involuntarily hospitalized if the client is not willing to be hospitalized voluntarily. Based on a statute in many states referred to as the Tarasoff ruling, therapists also have a duty to warn the intended victim of the potential homicide. For example, if a client reports that he is going to kill his ex-wife and he is involuntarily hospitalized because he is dangerous, the therapist must break confidentiality to inform the ex-wife of the client's threats against her. This ruling is based on a tragic case in California where the intended victim was not warned and was murdered after the ex-boyfriend was released from jail. Only in the most extreme cases do therapists need to contact the police or have their client involuntarily hospitalized because of threatened harm to another. At some point in their lives many people harbor intense angry feelings that lead them to wish death upon another person. It is the therapist's responsibility to break confidentiality only in those extreme cases where the homicidal wishes seem likely to be carried out.

In the case of physical abuse or neglect of a child, an incapacitated adult (such as a severely developmentally delayed adult), or an incapacitated elderly person, therapists are mandated to break confidentiality in order to report to the appropriate governing agency their strong suspicions of abuse. In these cases, the governing agency, usually the child protective agency discussed above for children or the adult protective agency for reporting abuse of an incapacitated adult or an elderly adult, conducts an investigation into the allegations of abuse and responds accordingly.

A similar process occurs for strong suspicions of sexual abuse of a child. If a therapist suspects that a child is being sexually abused (regardless of whether or not the child or the alleged perpetrator is the client), therapists have a duty to report their suspicions to the child protective agency that will then investigate the allegations.

All these limits to confidentiality are intended to prevent suicide, homicide, physical abuse, and sexual abuse from occurring. These ethical guidelines and laws were set up to protect people from themselves and from others.

Turning from the limits to confidentiality to the maintenance of confidentiality, an interesting issue often arises when children, families, and couples are involved in therapy. Recall that information shared between the therapist and the client is confidential and cannot be shared except in the rare cases just mentioned. When only one person is involved in therapy, such as with an individual adult client, the rules of confidentiality are clear-cut—nothing the client says ever goes beyond the therapist. But when more than one person is "the client," as, for example, in therapy for children, families, and couples, how is information shared or not shared with different members of the therapeutic unit? What if a 14-year-old privately tells the therapist that he drinks one beer each night before he goes to sleep but asks the therapist not to tell his parents? What if, in an individual meeting with the therapist who is conducting marital therapy, a wife reports to the therapist that she is having an affair but does not want her husband to be told? Unfortunately, these questions have no easy answers; there are no set standards by which to answer them. The only rule therapists must observe is to set confidentiality rules at the beginning of therapy and inform all participants, including children, mothers, fathers, stepmothers, and stepfathers, what rules of confidentiality will be followed. If the family members do not agree with the rules of confidentiality, they can negotiate with the therapist for rules that everyone in the family can agree upon, or they can choose to find another therapist who has rules of confidentiality consistent with their own wishes.

Different therapists choose to observe different rules of confidentiality when treating families and couples. For example, some therapists may choose to say that anything told to them by a client apart from other family will remain private between the therapist and that client (with the exceptions of the limits to confidentiality already discussed). In these cases, assuming the behavior did not fall into the danger to self limit to confidentiality, the therapist would have to keep the teenager's drinking a secret from the parents and would have to keep the wife's affair secret from the husband. Therapists in these cases might work with the teenager or the wife to help them find the strength to share this information with their parents or husband, respectively, but the therapist could not change the rules of confidentiality because new information was learned. If the therapist had chosen to say that nothing is confidential or secret between family members but is confidential outside the family unit, then the therapist could report the alcohol use to the parents and could report the extramarital affair to the husband if doing so would be therapeutic.

To set specific rules of confidentiality within families and couples is a difficult clinical decision. Most of the time, the decision depends on the age of the child and the therapist's own orientation. For example, some therapists will not meet with an individual from couple's therapy unless the other member of the couple is present. The guideline most often followed is that any disclosure within couple's therapy is fair game for the other member of the couple to know; in this approach, the therapist does not want to be in the position of inadvertently colluding with one member of the couple. When working with children and especially teenagers, however, in general, information told to the therapist remains between the therapist and the individual family member unless the disclosure falls within the limits to confidentiality. With teenagers, this approach is used because it is important that teenagers be able to trust the therapist and to express their innermost concerns. If they thought that everything would automatically be reported to their parents, teens might not disclose information important for the therapist to know. Conversely, if teenagers felt free to share everything with their therapist, and if the therapist could work cooperatively with teenage clients so that eventually important concerns could be shared with the parents directly, the result would be a win-win situation.

Obviously, these are difficult issues that require a lot of clinical training and a lot of thought to resolve. It is important that family members ask the therapist about who will have access to what information and under what conditions. If family members feel uncomfortable with the rules of confidentiality that have been described by the therapist, they should discuss their concerns with the therapist. If their concerns are still not addressed, then they may want to seek a therapist more consistent with their line of thinking.

SUMMARY

There are many therapists in every community and many types of therapy for any problem that exists. Family members are encouraged to find help that allows them to feel safe and that gives them hope for changing behaviors that need to be changed. It takes a lot of courage to reach out to find help for your own or your family's problems, but most people find that therapy can alleviate months and sometimes years of emotional suffering.

7

ENCOURAGING MENTAL HEALTH IN FAMILIES OF THE FUTURE

Sticks in a bundle are unbreakable.

—PROVERB OF AFRICA

It is ironic that many people harken back to the good old days reflected in *The Brady Bunch* television series without remembering that *The Brady Bunch* was created by two single parents marrying and creating a large blended family. To lament today's changing family constellations is neither useful nor productive. What is productive is to find ways for parents and children to maintain positive family bonds whether or not they live in the same household. The following suggestions apply to many types of families with children of all ages. Obviously, different parenting behaviors and family activities are appropriate for children of different ages. There are, however, common themes that can help to develop and to maintain good mental health in parents and children of all ages.

AUTHORITATIVE PARENTING: PROVIDING WARMTH AND RATIONAL CONTROL

As discussed throughout this book, the parenting style most closely associated with psychologically healthy children is authoritative parenting. Parents with this parenting style provide their children with age-appropriate structure and rules and a great deal of warmth and love. Whenever we talk about parenting behaviors, it is important to consider the age of the child; hence the focus on age-appropriate behaviors. For example, if it is cold and snowing, most parents know there are different strategies for bundling up their child, depending on the age of the child. Parents of infants automatically bundle up their infants themselves; they don't ask their infants what they want to wear. Parents of toddlers know not to ask their toddlers whether they want to wear a coat but, rather, to ask something like "Do you want to wear the red coat or the blue coat?" This way the toddlers have choices realistic for their age. Parents of 8- or 9-year-old children may just have to provide a reminder about putting something on (e.g., as the children are rushing to their rooms to get their ice skates, the parent might remind them to put on their favorite jacket). Finally, if all goes well, parents of teenagers may just smile as they see their teenagers bolt out the door with a coat on and ice hockey sticks trailing behind (of course, there are some teenagers that may still need the occasional, or even constant, reminder).

Overall, providing structure and love to children has been found to be effective regardless of whether the parent is a father or a mother. This type of structure and warmth is most helpful if provided on a consistent basis, whether or not the parents live together. There will almost always be differences in the ways that fathers and mothers interact with their children, but the more parents try to coordinate their efforts, the more they are parenting with their children's best interests in mind.

ACTIONS SPEAK LOUDER THAN WORDS

The old idea of "Do as I say, not as I do" just does not work in most instances. Children of all ages observe how their parents behave and model their own behavior after their parents in at least some way. Parents who feel happy with their own behavior—especially in controlling anger, dealing with conflict, and demonstrating personal habits such as reading books, exercising, eating healthy foods, not smoking, and not abusing legal or illegal drugs—are probably pleased to learn that at some level their children will be following in their footsteps. Parents who are less than pleased with their own behavior are probably less than pleased to learn that they are inadvertently teaching their children the wrong lessons.

Countless times I have heard parents screaming at their child for yelling at someone else or I hear about parents who spank their children because the children have hit someone else. Sometimes it seems most appropriate to hold up a mirror to the parents and suggest that they look at themselves in order to understand where the child learned some of these bad behaviors. This is not to say that children pick up bad habits only from their parents, nor is it to say that parents who live an honorable lifestyle will not have to deal with problem behavior in their children. Children can learn bad behavior (as well as good behavior) from a number of sources, including their friends, other children at school, other children's parents, teachers, and characters on television, in the movies, and in books. It is to say, however, that children are like sponges who soak up the environment around them. Because this is so, it is incumbent upon parents to make the environment one with which they wish their children to be saturated.

RESOLVE CONFLICT AND DON'T PUT CHILDREN IN THE MIDDLE

Given that children often do what their parents do, it is important to highlight that youngsters often learn how to deal with anger and conflict by watching how their parents deal with anger and conflict. One of the lessons taught in behavioral parent training is that parents should not spank their children out of anger. Based on this model, if parents use spanking as a form of punishment, it should be done in a controlled manner (such as calmly explaining why the child is being punished and applying only two swats with an open hand to the child's clothed bottom). Some parents who use corporal punishment (i.e., spanking) might be rolling their eyes right now and saying, "Yeah, right." But think about it: If parents hit their children when they are angry, then it is not surprising that their children learn to hit others when they are angry. Commonly, preschoolers and kindergartners are told to "use words rather than fists" to get their point across. Many adults can learn from these lessons too—both in their behavior with their children and in their behavior with other adults.[1]

As for children and the use of spanking, I should mention that a great deal of professionals do not condone the use of spanking at all. A number of studies have suggested that spanking as the primary mechanism for punishment only teaches children what not to do rather than teaching them what to do. Further, spanking often leads to fear of the adult who is doing the spanking. In addition, children who are spanked tend to be more aggressive than children who are not spanked. For these reasons, many professionals suggest that other methods of teaching appropriate behavior should be used; these methods include paying attention to good behavior, rewarding children for good behavior (with rewards ranging from monetary or gift rewards to a pat on the back or a hug), ignoring certain bad behavior (such as not responding to children when they are whining, but responding immediately to them once they stop whining), using natural consequences to some inappropriate behaviors (such as letting children play roughly with a toy that they had been warned about and then allowing them to deal with the consequences of having a toy that was broken as a result of their rough playing style), and using time-out for inappropriate behavior. Parents who wish to learn more about effective parenting behaviors are encouraged to seek out professional help as well as to find appropriate popular books on parenting, such as *Touchpoints: The Essential Reference, Raising Black Children, Systematic Training for Effective Parenting: The Parent's Handbook, How to Talk So Kids Will Listen and Listen So Kids Will Talk, Parenting for Dummies,* and *Teen Tips: A Practical Survival Guide for Parents with Kids 11 to 19.* There are also books for parents with specialized needs, such as *Growing up with Divorce: Helping Your Child Avoid Immediate and Later Emotional Problems, The Single Parent's Almanac: Real-World Answers to Everyday Questions, Mom's House, Dad's House: Making Shared Custody Work,* and *Grandparents as Parents: A Survival Guide for Raising a Second Family.*[2]

In addition to handling anger appropriately with their children, parents must learn how to deal appropriately when angry with other adults. No matter how much any two people try to prevent conflict, some conflict is always bound to arise. One of the most important things, as far as children are concerned, is that children should not be put in the middle of their parents' arguments or discussions. This suggestion goes for parents who are still married to each other as well as for parents who are no longer together. The term "triangulation" is used to refer to situations in which children are put in between their parents or are used as a pawn by one parent against the other parent. Triangulation occurs, for example, when parents having a disagreement with each other try to elicit the support of their children or try to convince their children that they are right and the other parent is wrong. Triangulation is associated with a number of emotional and behavioral problems in children, adolescents, and adult children and should therefore be avoided whenever possible.[3]

Even when children are not put between their arguing parents, parental arguing remains harmful to children. Many times parents say hurtful things to each other in the heat of an argument and then make up for the argument behind closed doors. If children see and hear only the hurtful part of arguing but are not able to learn how to resolve conflict, then it is difficult for them to resolve conflict when it comes up in their own lives. In general, conflict and arguing should be kept away from children as much as possible. When conflict does arise, children must understand how to deal with conflict in a nondestructive and even productive manner. Some parents may need to learn these skills for themselves before they can hope to pass these skills on to their children.

STAYING APART WHEN YOU'RE CLOSE

Different families have different levels of closeness with which they are comfortable. From a family therapy perspective, if family members are too emotionally distant from one another, the family is "disengaged." At the other end of the continuum, if family members are too emotionally involved with one another, the family is "enmeshed." A primary criticism of theories regarding family functioning in the United States is that "healthy families" have been defined with a Caucasian, European American family in mind. This model of a healthy family suggests that family members have a certain degree of closeness, but also that individuals maintain a fair amount of individuality and separateness from their family. A number of writers have noted that this ideal of a family is not consistent with families from all walks of life. For example, Cuban American families and Italian American families tend to value closeness and emotional expression more than do most Caucasian American families of European heritage. In addition, different families define "family" in different ways. For example, whereas Caucasian Americans of European heritage usually define a family based on the nuclear family, African American families often focus more on a kinship and community network, and Chinese American families often focus on multiple generations, including ancestors and descendants, when considering their family. Overall, there are a number of different goals and definitions that different families may have for themselves. The important thing is for families to try to reach these goals as a unit and as individuals.[4]

If at least some sense of individuality and separateness is a goal for members within a family, individuals must be allowed to grow as a person as well as a family member. For many parents, this means they need to develop or maintain friendships outside the family and to continue to pursue individual interests such as educational goals, artistic adventures, athletic pursuits, or spiritual goals. A number of books can help individuals pursue their interests. One book that can help individuals identify their own interests is *The Artist's Way*.[5]

In addition to growing as an individual, growing as a couple or finding a partner with whom to grow if the parent is currently single is important for parents. Family theorists have long discussed the need for a stable and happy parental relationship in order to maintain a healthy family environment for children. If parents are no longer involved with each other, then the same importance can be focused upon the parents' individual romantic relationships with another partner. Just as children learn from their parents how to negotiate conflict and anger, they also learn how to develop and maintain satisfying adult relationships (e.g., do the partners seem to respect each other, do they seem to share joyful experiences with each other, do they support each other during stressful times, do they tolerate each other's irritating habits, and do they work together as a team). Obviously, many conversations and activities between adults need to be kept away from children, but parents who are happy in their own romantic relationship can often be happier in their role as a parent.[6]

It is important for parents as individuals as well as parents as part of a couple not to allow themselves to become isolated because of family duties necessary on a daily basis. How many parents are faced with needing to rush home from work, fix dinner, and then get their children to soccer practice, then to ballet rehearsal, and then to marching band practice all in one evening? The daily demands of a busy family's schedule are daunting, and it is easy for parents swept up by their children's social needs to forget their own social needs. One way many parents can help themselves and each other is to connect with other parents whose children are involved in the same activities. Given that many of these parents may be in the same life situation (e.g., busy schedules, children of the same age, and similar struggles between energy for work and family), parents may be able to develop support networks and friendships with other parents. Many parents also find support through their religious or community organizations. Regardless of the mechanism, parents need to find social support for themselves so that they do not feel isolated by the heavy demands of parenthood.

STAYING CLOSE WHEN YOU'RE APART

On the other end of the continuum of losing your own identity within the family is not having an identity within the family. Specifically, many parents who do not live with their children often feel left out of their children's lives. As discussed in the first chapter, many fathers who were close to their children before the divorce seem to disengage from their children after the divorce because it is so painful for them to try to maintain a less intense parenting role. Many noncustodial fathers and mothers, however, do not intentionally remove themselves from their children's lives; instead, they find that their relationship with their child becomes distant over time.[7]

Although having a child visit you only occasionally is unquestionably different than living with a child full time, there are a number of activities noncustodial parents can try in order to maintain a strong relationship with their children. As well as considering the suggestions made in the following pages of this book, noncustodial fathers may want to go to their local bookstore or library to pick up a copy of *Fathering: Strengthening Connection with Your Children No Matter Where You Are*, which provides a number of ideas on ways to maintain the father-child relationship.[8]

Consistency of Contact

One of the bottom lines in parenting, whether or not your children live with you, is to be consistent in how you treat your children and in the type of environment you provide for them. Based on object relations theory (a psychodynamic or Freudian theory), infants learn about the world through the consistency of their caretakers. If the caretaker responds to their cries and responds to their needs in relatively the same way each time, then the infant learns that the world is a safe place. This theory goes on to suggest that infants who are given secure environments from early in their lives will grow up to seek out stable and secure environments as they get older. This type of consistency is also important during childhood and adolescence.[9]

How this consistency relates to noncustodial parents should be obvious. If a noncustodial parent is scheduled to have the children visit on alternating Wednesday nights and every other weekend, then the noncustodial parent should make sure to maintain this visitation schedule if at all feasible. Obviously, plans have to be changed sometimes, but the more consistency you can provide for your children, the more secure they will feel in their relationship with you. This same consistency should be maintained for other activities like phone calls, holiday celebrations, and birthday celebrations.

You might even recall when you were a child and someone promised you something but then did not follow through on the promise. Depending on the age and the circumstances, children can be devastated by broken promises, and a series of broken promises can lead to a broken parent-child relationship. From these visitations children take fundamental messages about trust and love. It is therefore critically important to convey your feelings accurately—if your children really are important to you, then make your commitments to them a priority. Children also place a great deal of importance on the activities in which they are involved. If your daughter really loves softball, then show interest in her softball game—either by attending the game if you live in the same area or by asking about it if you live far away. Similarly, if your son has hopes of going to college on a drama scholarship, then attending his play at school or calling right after the play is over would be terribly important. For most parents, what is important to their children is important to them. Some parents have to work harder at developing interest in their children's activities, but this interest can go a long way toward maintaining a strong parent-child relationship.

Common Experiences

In addition to developing interest in your children's interests, noncustodial parents can benefit from finding ways to have experiences in common with their children. Much of what changes when a parent no longer lives with his or her child is the day-to-day experiences of life (e.g., eating dinner together, playing with the dog, having quiet time to do homework or to read, watching sports on television, or driving to the video store to rent movies). Although many families who live under the same roof have also lost these common experiences, these experiences are particularly missing from the daily experience of noncustodial parents.

Because these daily routines can help maintain a strong parent-child bond, many noncustodial parents have tried to find ways of developing opportunities to share such common experiences. I knew of a noncustodial father who lived over 500 miles from his son, but who wanted to maintain relatively regular contact with his son. In addition to monthly weekend visits, the father would call the son twice a week at regularly scheduled times and they would watch a television show together over the phone. They would talk before and after the show and during commercials, and then they would comment on the show to each other as they were watching it. Although not everyone can afford the resulting airplane and phone bills, this example illustrates a creative way to maintain contact with children who do not live with you. It also illustrates that cooperation between parents is necessary to enable both parents to maintain a relationship with their children. The mother in this scenario was supportive of the son watching these shows with his father, and she was pleased to see her son's enjoyment of his father's attention.

There are many less expensive ways to develop and maintain common experiences between noncustodial parents and children. Writing letters and choosing interesting stamps for the envelopes can be one way to maintain a relationship with your child. If you and your child have access to computers and electronic mail, then e-mail is a wonderful way of maintaining daily contact. Through e-mail you could even share tips on interesting places to visit on the World Wide Web. The same sharing of common experiences goes for other activities, such as sporting events, movies, books, nature, hobbies, and music. I know of more than one nighttime phone conversation where both parent and child were miles apart but were outside looking at the same moon and commenting on their common experience of it. If the parents and children live in the same town, then such common experiences could be even more easily achieved. Developing and maintaining common experiences requires creativity and energy, but the increased closeness between parents and children can be well worth the effort.

Make Room in Your Life

All the suggestions on how to maintain contact with your children take time and energy. The need for time and energy devoted to your children is necessary whether or not your children live with you. As with most adults, most children do best in environments in which they feel wanted and appreciated. It is helpful if children can feel they have their own "space" in the house they visit. Sometimes it is not feasible for children to have their own room, especially if they stay in it only four or five days a month, but the more you can provide a sense of permanence and belonging for your child, the better. Allowing your children to keep certain items of clothing or certain toys with their visiting parent might help them feel that they are at a home away from home. Given that pets are so important to children as well as to many adults, noncustodial parents may want to consider allowing the child's pet to visit as well, or they may consider getting a pet to keep for the child. Consistent activities during visitations can also help the child feel safe and secure (e.g., a special meal together on one of the nights or a favorite activity that can become part of the routine).

How noncustodial parents spend their time with their children will change as the child grows older, of course. As children get closer to the teenage years, they start wanting to spend time in their own activities and with their own friends. It is important that custodial and noncustodial parents help their children find a balance between independence from the family and interconnection within the family. If parents have been modeling these behaviors all along, their child can learn how to balance these competing demands.

BE HERE NOW

The classic Buddhist saying "Be here now" can be used to refer to individuals themselves, but it also can be applied to the parent-child relationship in single-parent and dual-parent households. How often have you seen a child excitedly telling his or her parent a long and involved story to which the parent responds, "Go on, I'm listening," while the parent is obviously attending to something else? It is not realistic to expect parents to listen intently to every word their child utters, nor is it realistic to expect children to listen intently to every word their parent utters. It is, however, realistic for parents to try to focus on their children when they can and for parents to make time to listen to their children.

As discussed in the first chapter, there is a difference between the physical presence of a parent and the psychological or emotional presence of a parent. Being psychologically and emotionally present and available for your children means that you are attending to them, that you are supportive of their concerns, and that you are there for them. Some people may refer to psychological and emotional presence with their children as "quality time" with their children. The mere physical presence with children is not especially helpful for psychological development if a parent is not responsive to his or her child's interests and actions.[10]

"Be here now" can be achieved in a number of ways, but first a little self-appraisal is in order. Are you nearly always doing something else (such as watching television, reading the newspaper, doing the dishes, cooking, doing yardwork, or paying bills) when you are with your children? Do you often find that you were not paying attention to what your child was saying and that you are unable to answer your child's question when it relates to what he or she was saying? Do you often have no idea who your child's friends are? Do you often find yourself thinking about work or trying to solve work problems mentally when you are with your child? Do you find that your child has to scream "Mom" or "Dad" a number of times to get your attention because you were engaged in other activities when you were with him or her? "Yes" answers to these questions suggest a parent who is not actively attending to his or her children.

Given the demands of running a household, being employed part or full time, trying to maintain a marriage or a romantic relationship, and raising children, it is unrealistic to expect that all parents will completely concentrate on their children when spending time with them. But if there is also no time during the day when the child is the complete focus of parents' attention, then problems in the parent-child relationship may develop.

A first step to practicing attention on your child comes from an exercise done near the beginning of behavioral parent training. Try identifying 15 to 20 minutes per day for one week during which you will just focus on your child and on nothing else. The suggestion is to let your child define the activities; you are not allowed to try to control the situation unless it is for reasons of safety. For younger children, the child might choose to play a game or have a story read. Older children may want to play a video game with you or discuss a particular topic. The idea is for you to focus solely on the child and the child's needs. Many parents already have this type of activity built naturally into their own family schedules. Some parents, however, are surprised at how difficult they find this activity.[11]

After completing these activities for a week with each child, the idea is to find ways to integrate "quality time" with your children into your daily schedules. For many families, a sit-down dinner with the entire family present is a way to focus on each other and build on common experiences. For other families, there might be a favorite activity such as fishing or hiking that allows quality parent-child interactions. One of the tasks in my own research with parents and 11- to-18-year-olds is for the mother and the father to each have a five-minute conversation alone with their teenager. It is surprising how many families have difficulty with finding things to talk about to fill up five minutes. A number of parents have commented that they did not realize how little they actually talked with their teenager. For some families, having quality time in which parents are there for their children is such a foreign idea that parents may become nervous even trying to get close to their children. If parents feel that they cannot even talk with their own children, then professional help is probably advised. Even the most well behaved teenagers can be difficult to talk with sometimes, but if they were raised without much of a parent-child connection, then more than just "quality time" may be necessary to build a bond between parent and teenager.

STEPPING INTO A FAMILY

One of the more controversial areas for family therapists is knowing what to recommend to stepparents and their partners. The role of a stepparent varies widely depending on the age of the child, the living situation, and the expectations of caretaking responsibilities. In general, the younger the child is and the more time the stepparent will spend with the child, the more caretaking responsibilities the stepparent should try to take on. Because older children and teenagers often dismiss any caretaking activities from a stepparent, it is often helpful for the stepparent to take on a nonparenting role that is primarily friendly in nature. Regardless of the age of the child, adult dyads (e.g., the parent and stepparent or the parent and significant other) must remain united and supportive of the caretaking decisions made by the other partner. If parents and stepparents disagree with each other about how to handle the children, they should discuss the issues away from the children. Discussions between ex-spouses and current spouses can also be tricky to maneuver, so these discussions should also be held away from the children until a sense of equilibrium has been achieved.

The joining of different family units, as in blended families, can be difficult and becomes especially complicated when both partners have children from previous relationships. The best overall advice family therapists can give is to suggest that good parenting also applies to good stepparenting: Try to have the parental unit act as a unit. Try to provide warmth and structure consistent with what is already being done in the household. Try to keep conflict away from the children. Try to be psychologically and emotionally present for the children. Try to maintain your own mental health. Although we all hear horror stories of evil stepparents (yet again stepmothers have received most of the bad rap on this one), and we have all heard horror stories of chaotic stepfamily situations, many stepfamilies do find a way to live together in relative harmony. Interested readers may want to drop by their local bookstore or library to find more information on stepfamilies. Two particularly good books on the subject are *Step-by-Stepparenting: A Guide to Successful Living with a Blended Family* and *Strengthening Your Stepfamily*. In the best of all worlds, the joining together of two families illustrates the classic concept from Gestalt psychology that the whole can be greater than the sum of its parts.[12]

THE PERSONAL IS POLITICAL

Much of the focus of this chapter has been on what parents can do to help their relationship with their children and with other family members and friends. It should also be emphasized that families do not exist in isolation; there are important political and social factors to consider that affect the well-being of families. The Family and Medical Leave Act has gone a long way to protect workers' rights when they need to attend to family duties. There are, however, a number of other issues that parents may want to consider in their professional lives, issues related to their personal well-being and the well-being of their family.

When a single parent who is running the household is employed or even when both parents are employed, day care is often a necessity. Given that so many people live away from their family of origin, the extended family network cannot be relied upon to provide child care when parents are employed. I have yet to meet an employed parent who has not struggled with the issues surrounding day care for his or her children. Issues include such things as quality of the day care staff and setting, safety of the children while at day care, the often exorbitant cost of high-quality day care facilities, in-home versus out-of-home care, the possibility of flexible schedules to maximize parent contact with the children, and guilt over leaving children with another caretaker. It is unfortunate when parents have to struggle with these issues, but it seems likely that if parents as voters and citizens mobilized to make affordable, high-quality day care a priority, then there might be less of a struggle. The same can be said for work schedules and job requirements that can be made more family-friendly. Day care and the workplace exist as they do today because we have either actively created them that way or passively allowed them to become that way. In either case, once you have worked out an arrangement that keeps your own family safe and happy, you may want to consider taking action to help other families find safety and happiness with a little less of a struggle. For other thoughts on the importance of making children and families a personal and political priority, you are encouraged to read the powerful and inspirational book *It Takes a Village and Other Lessons Children Teach Us* by Hillary Rodham Clinton and the equally powerful and inspirational book by Marian Wright Edelman entitled *The Measure of Our Success*. For strategies to get men more involved in children's lives in a responsible manner, you are encouraged to read *Getting Men Involved: Strategies for Early Childhood Programs* and *New Expectations: Community Strategies for Responsible Fatherhood*.[13]

PREVENTING PROBLEMS (NOT JUST REACTING TO PROBLEMS)

The old saying "An ounce of prevention is worth a pound of cure" is relevant to parents' and children's mental health. Regarding children, it is in children's and parents' best interests to prevent problems from occurring rather than only reacting to problems when they occur. I find it heartbreaking to hear from parents of teenagers who are at their wits' end with their teenager's behavior but who have never before sought professional help. It is never too late to seek help, but the earlier that problems are addressed, the better the outcome in most cases. The other heartbreaking pattern that often occurs in therapy is that once there is some improvement in a child's or teenager's behavior, parents stop bringing their child to therapy. Often they discontinue therapy too early, only to have the problems reappear later. Except in cases of trauma, such as sexual assault of a child or the death of a loved one, rarely do children's problem behaviors develop overnight. It is also rare that these problems can be alleviated overnight.

The same patterns hold true for mental health problems in parents. Parents who deal with their own mental health problems in therapy, consequently prevent their children from having to experience the negative consequences of having a psychologically distressed parent. Preventing problems from occurring in both children and parents can save a great deal of psychological pain and distress in the long run.

TAKING RESPONSIBILITY

In the Introduction, I made reference to one of my favorite post-reunion Eagles songs called "Get over It." Songs can always have different meanings for different people, but to me, this song should be the anthem for all of us to take more personal responsibility. Too often these days people want to look everywhere else but in themselves to find fault and to identify the reasons for why they are unhappy. Although it is often the case that there are legitimate and "blameworthy" others—adults who sexually or physically abuse a child, for example, or parents who intentionally emotionally abuse their children or who abuse each other—rarely do individuals not have some control over the predicaments in which they find themselves. Perhaps they were not raised by the most caring and sensitive parents. Perhaps their favorite blanket was taken away from them when they were 3 years old. Perhaps they have had to struggle twice as much as others to get half as much. No matter what cards individuals have been dealt in life, it is important that they take stock of what part of their life is within their control and then do something about it. It is terribly sad when people lament the state of their life but then do nothing to try to improve their life. To maintain a happy and productive life takes hard work, but the hard work is usually worth it.

SUMMARY

How interesting that a book on fathers should end with a chapter that focuses on families rather than just on fathers. In some ways, that is the point of this book. As much as we see differences in the ways fathers and mothers treat their children, there are far more similarities than differences. Good parenting is good parenting—whether it is provided by the father, the mother, the grandmother who now has custody, the ex-boyfriend of the incarcerated mother, or another primary caretaker who is unrelated to the child. Mental health problems in children can influence and can be influenced by fathers and mothers in surprisingly similar ways. Rather than creating more chasms between fathers and mothers, men and women, these findings of similarities confirm that we are all in the same boat and that paddling together is much easier than paddling separately. Let's just hope that we're not heading upstream.

Appendix

———————————•———————————

ORGANIZATIONS: SUPPORT GROUPS

Children and Adults with Attention Deficit Disorders
(CHADD: Support groups)
      499 Northwest 70th Avenue, Suite 109
      Plantation, FL 33317
      (305) 587-3700

Learning Disorder Association of America
(LDA: Support groups and referrals)
      4156 Library Road
      Pittsburgh, PA 15234
      (412) 341-1515

Parents Anonymous
(Hotline and referrals for parents who are under stress)
      6733 S. Sepulveda Boulevard., Suite 270
      Los Angeles, CA 90045

(800) 421-0353 in all states except California
(800) 352-0386 in California

Parents without Partners (Support groups)
    401 N. Michigan Avenue
    Chicago, IL 60611
    (800) 637-7974

ORGANIZATIONS: SOCIAL, POLITICAL, AND PROFESSIONAL

The Fatherhood Project (Network for fathers and professionals)
    Families and Work Institute
    330 Seventh Avenue
    New York, NY 10001
    (212) 465-2044

National Center for Family-Centered Care
(Publishes newsletter: National Fathers Network Newsletter)
    7910 Woodmont Avenue, Suite 300
    Bethesda, MD 20814
    (301) 654-6549

National Fatherhood Initiative
(For encouragement of responsible fatherhood)
    600 Eden Road, Building E
    Lancaster, PA 17601
    (717) 581-8860

National Center on Fathers and Families
(Network for professionals)
    University of Pennsylvania
    Graduate School of Education
    3700 Walnut Street, Box 58
    Philadelphia, PA 19104-6216
    (215) 573-5500

NOTES

●

INTRODUCTION

1. L. B. Braverman, "Beyond the myth of motherhood," in M. McGoldrick, C. M. Anderson, and F. Walsh (eds.), *Women and families* (New York: Free Press, 1989), pp. 227–243; S. Coontz, *The way we never were: American families and the nostalgia trap* (New York: Basic Books, 1992); S. Scarr, D. Phillips, and K. McCartney, "Working mothers and their families," *American Psychologist, 44* (1989): 1402–1409; L. Thompson and A. J. Walker, "Gender in families: Women and men in marriage, work, and parenthood," *Journal of Marriage and the Family, 51* (1989): 845–871.

CHAPTER 1

1. D. Blankenhorn, *Fatherless America: Confronting our most urgent social problem* (New York: Basic Books, 1995); D. Popenoe, *Life without father: Compelling new evidence that fatherhood and marriage are indispensable for the good of children and society* (New York: Free

Press, 1996); S. Roberts, *Who we are: A portrait of America based on the latest U.S. Census* (New York: Random House, 1993); J. A. Seltzer and Y. Brandreth, "What fathers say about involvement with children after separation," *Journal of Family Issues, 14* (1994): 49–77.

2. S. Roberts, *Who we are: A portrait of America based on the latest U.S. Census* (New York: Random House, 1993).

3. J. A. Seltzer and S. M. Bianchi, "Children's contact with absent parents," *Journal of Marriage and the Family, 50* (1988): 663–677; J. A. Seltzer and Y. Brandreth, "What fathers say about involvement with children after separation," *Journal of Family Issues, 14* (1994): 49–77.

4. M. E. Lamb (ed.), *The role of the father in child development* (3rd ed.) (New York: Wiley, 1997).

5. L. Thompson and A. J. Walker, "Gender in families: Women and men in marriage, work, and parenthood," *Journal of Marriage and the Family, 51* (1989): 845–871.

6. The information on the father's role in normal development that is discussed in this chapter can be found in M. E. Lamb (ed.), *The role of the father in child development* (3rd ed.) (New York: Wiley, 1997).

7. C. P. Cowan and P. A. Cowan, "Who does what when partners become parents: Implications for men, women, and marriage," *Marriage and Family Review, 12* (1988): 105–131; P. Daniels and K. Weingarten, "The fatherhood click: The timing of parenthood in men's lives," in P. Bronstein and C. P. Cowan (eds.), *Fatherhood today: Men's changing role in the family* (New York: Wiley, 1988), pp. 36–52; B. I. Fagot and R. Hagan, "Observations of parent reactions to sex-stereotyped behaviors: Age and sex effects," *Child Development, 62, (1991): 617–628; L. S. Fish, R. S. New, and N. J. VanCleave, "Shared parenting in dual-income families," American Journal of Orthopsychiatry, 62* (1992): 83–92; G. L. Greif and A. DeMaris, "Single fathers with custody," *Families in Society: The Journal of Contemporary Human Services, 71* (1990): 259–266; G. Russell, *The changing role of fathers?* (St. Lucia, Queensland, Australia: University of Queensland Press, 1983); L. B. Tiedje and C. S. Darling-Fisher, "Factors that influence fathers' participation in child care," *Health Care for Women International, 14* (1993): 99–107; M. W. Yogman, J. Cooley, and D. Kindlon, "Fathers, infants, and toddlers: A developing relationship," in P. Bronstein and C. P. Cowan (eds.), *Fatherhood today: Men's changing role in the family* (New York: Wiley, 1988), pp. 53–65.

8. L. Thompson and A. J. Walker, "Gender in families: Women and men in marriage, work, and parenthood," *Journal of Marriage and the Family, 51* (1989): 845–871.

9. R. C. Barnett and G. K. Baruch, "Determinants of fathers' participation in family work," *Journal of Marriage and the Family, 49* (1987): 29–40; M. E. Lamb (ed.), *The role of the father in child development* (3rd ed.) (New York: Wiley, 1997); W. Marsiglio, "Paternal engagement activities with minor children," *Journal of Marriage and the Family, 53* (1991): 973–986; F. L. Mott, "Sons, daughters and fathers' absence: Differentials in father-leaving probabilities and in home environments," *Journal of Family Issues, 14* (1994): 97–128; M. E. Starrels, "Gender differences in parent-child relations," *Journal of Family Issues, 14* (1994): 148–165.

10. M. E. Lamb (ed.), *The father's role: Applied perspectives* (New York: Wiley, 1986); G. A. Morelli and E. Z. Tronick, "Efe fathers: One among many? A comparison of forager children's involvement with fathers and other males," *Social Development, 1* (1992): 36–54; M. N. Wilson, T.F.J. Tolson, I. D. Hinton, and M. Kiernan, "Flexibility and sharing of childcare duties in black families," *Sex Roles, 22* (1990): 409–425.

11. F. K. Grossman, W. S. Pollack, and E. Golding, "Fathers and children: Predicting the quality and quantity of fathering," *Developmental Psychology, 24* (1988): 82–91.

12. L. B. Braverman, "Beyond the myth of motherhood," in M. McGoldrick, C. M. Anderson, and F. Walsh (eds.), *Women and families* (New York: Free Press, 1989), pp. 227–243; S. Scarr, D. Phillips, and K. McCartney, "Working mothers and their families," *American Psychologist, 44* (1989): 1402–1409; L. Thompson and A. J. Walker, "Gender in families: Women and men in marriage, work, and parenthood," *Journal of Marriage and the Family, 51* (1989): 845–871.

13. S. Roberts, *Who we are: A portrait of America based on the latest U.S. Census* (New York: Random House, 1993).

14. J. A. Seltzer and Y. Brandreth, "What fathers say about involvement with children after separation," *Journal of Family Issues, 14* (1994): 49–77.

15. F. L. Mott, "When is a father really gone? Paternal-child contact in father-absent homes," *Demography, 27* (1990): 499–517.

16. E. Anderson, *Streetwise: Race, class, and change in an urban community* (Chicago: University of Chicago Press, 1990).

17. C. R. Ahrons and R. B. Miller, "The effect of the postdivorce relationship on paternal involvement: A longitudinal analysis,"

American Journal of Orthopsychiatry, 63 (1993): 441–450; P. C. McKenry, S. J. Price, M. A. Fine, and J. Serovich, "Predictors of single, noncustodial fathers' physical involvement with their children," *Journal of Genetic Psychology, 153* (1992): 305–319; J. Pearson and J. Anhalt, "Examining the connection between child access and child support," *Family and Conciliation Courts Review, 32* (1994): 93–109; J. A. Seltzer and Y. Brandreth, "What fathers say about involvement with children after separation," *Journal of Family Issues, 14* (1994): 49–77; J. C. Wall, "Maintaining the connection: Parenting as a noncustodial father," *Child and Adolescent Social Work Journal, 9* (1992): 441–456.

18. T. Arendell, *Fathers and divorce* (Thousand Oaks, CA: Sage Publications, 1995); E. Kruk, "The disengaged noncustodial father: Implications for social work practice with the divorced family," *Social Work, 39* (1994): 15–25.

19. J. M. Healy, J. E. Malley, and A. J. Stewart, "Children and their fathers after parental separation," *American Journal of Orthopsychiatry, 60* (1990): 531–543; J. A. Seltzer and S. M. Bianchi, "Children's contact with absent parents," *Journal of Marriage and the Family, 50* (1988): 663–677; L. B. Silverstein, "Primate research, family politics, and social policy: Transforming 'cads' into 'dads,'" *Journal of Family Psychology, 7* (1993): 267–282.

20. R. Forehand, M. Wierson, A. M. Thomas, L. Armistead, T. Kempton, and R. Fauber, "Interparental conflict and paternal visitation following divorce: The interactive effect on adolescent competence," *Child Study Journal, 20* (1990): 193–202.

21. E. M. Cummings and P. Davies, *Children and marital conflict: The impact of family dispute and resolution* (New York: Guilford Press, 1994).

22. J. A. Seltzer and Y. Brandreth, "What fathers say about involvement with children after separation," *Journal of Family Issues, 14* (1994): 49–77; U.S. Bureau of the Census, *Households, families, and children: A 30–year perspective* (Washington, DC: U.S. Government Printing Office, 1992), pp. 23–181.

23. R. E. Emery, S. G. Matthews, and M. M. Wyer, "Child custody mediation and litigation: Further evidence on the differing views of mothers and fathers," *Journal of Consulting and Clinical Psychology, 59* (1991): 410–418; L. J. Weitzman, "Women and children last: The social and economic consequences of divorce law reforms," in S. M. Dornbusch and M. H. Strober (eds.), *Feminism, children, and the new families* (New York: Guilford Press, 1988), pp. 212–248.

24. K. M. Paasch and J. D. Teachman, "Gender of children and receipt of assistance from absent fathers," *Journal of Family Issues, 12* (1991): 450–466; F. L. Sonenstein and C. A. Calhoun, "Determinants of child support: A pilot survey of absent parents," *Contemporary Policy Issues, 8* (1990): 75–94; U.S. Bureau of the Census, *Households, families, and children: A 30-year perspective* (Washington, DC: U.S. Government Printing Office, 1992), pp. 23–181.

25. W. Marsiglio, "Stepfathers with minor children living at home: Parenting perceptions and relationship quality," *Journal of Family Issues, 13* (1992): 195–214.

26. M. A. Fine, P. C. McKenry, B. W. Donnelly, and P. Voydanoff, "Perceived adjustment of parents and children: Variations by family structure, race, and gender," *Journal of Marriage and the Family, 54* (1992): 118–127; L. A. Kurdek and R. J. Sinclair, "Adjustment of young adolescents in two-parent nuclear, stepfather, and mother-custody families," *Journal of Consulting and Clinical Psychology, 56* (1988): 91–96.

27. G. L. Greif and A. DeMaris, "Single fathers with custody," *Families in Society: The Journal of Contemporary Human Services, 71* (1990): 259–266.

28. Ibid.

29. A. DeMaris and G. L. Greif, "The relationship between family structure and parent-child relationship problems in single father households," *Journal of Divorce and Remarriage, 18* (1992): 55–77; J. W. Santrock and R. A. Warshak, "Development, relationships, and legal/clinical considerations in father-custody families," in M. E. Lamb, *The father's role: Applied perspectives* (New York: Wiley, 1986), pp. 135–163; J. W. Santrock, R. A. Warshak, and G. L. Elliott, "Social development and parent-child interaction in father-custody and stepmother families," in M E. Lamb (ed.), *Nontraditional families: Parenting and child development* (Hillsdale, NJ: Lawrence Erlbaum, 1982), pp. 289–314.

30. S. Cullari and R. Mikus, "Correlates of adolescent sexual behavior," *Psychological Reports, 66* (1990): 1179–1184; R. J. Erickson and G. M. Babcock, "Men and family law: From patriarchy to partnership," *Marriage and Family Review, 21* (1995): 31–54; D. A. Hamburg, E. O. Nightingale, and R. Takanishi, "Facilitating the transitions of adolescence," *Journal of the American Medical Association, 257* (1987): 3405–3406.

31. R. J. Dworkin, J. T. Harding, and N. B. Schreiber, "Parenting or placing: Decision making by pregnant teens," *Youth and Society, 25* (1993): 75–92.

32. K. Dearden, C. Hale, and J. Alvarez, "The educational antecedents of teen fatherhood," *British Journal of Educational Psychology, 62* (1992): 139–147.

33. S. K. Danziger and N. Radin, "Absent does not equal uninvolved: Predictors of fathering in teen mother families," *Journal of Marriage and the Family, 52* (1990): 636–642.

34. K. Christmon, "Parental responsibility and self-image of African American fathers," *Families in Society: The Journal of Contemporary Human Services, 71* (1990): 563–567; K. Christmon, "Parental responsibility of African American unwed adolescent fathers," *Adolescence, 25* (1990): 645–653; J. L. McAdoo, "Understanding African-American teen fathers," in P. E. Leone (ed.), *Understanding troubled and troubling youth* (Beverly Hills, CA: Sage, 1990), pp. 229–245.

35. L. E. Hendricks, "Unwed adolescent fathers: Problems they face and their sources of social support," *Adolescence, 15* (1980): 860–869; J. L. McAdoo, "Understanding African-American teen fathers," in P. E. Leone (ed.), *Understanding troubled and troubling youth* (Beverly Hills, CA: Sage, 1990), pp. 229–245; M. S. Kiselica and P. Sturmer, "Is society giving teenage fathers a mixed message?" *Youth and Society, 24* (1993): 487–501; L. B. Silverstein, "Primate research, family politics, and social policy: Transforming 'cads' into 'dads,' " *Journal of Family Psychology, 7* (1993): 267–282.

36. J. M. Bailey, D. Bobrow, M. Wolfe, and S. Mikach, "Sexual orientation of adult sons of gay fathers," *Developmental Psychology, 31* (1995): 124–129; J. J. Bigner and R. B. Jacobsen, "Adult responses to child behavior and attitudes toward fathering: Gay and nongay fathers," *Journal of Homosexuality, 23* (1992): 99–112; F. W. Bozett (ed.), *Gay and lesbian parents* (New York: Praeger, 1987); C. J. Patterson, "Children of lesbian and gay parents," *Child Development, 63* (1992): 1025–1042.

37. E. M. Cummings and P. Davies, *Children and marital conflict: The impact of family dispute and resolution* (New York: Guilford Press, 1994); F. A. Pedersen, "Does research on children reared in father-absent families yield information on father influences?" *Family Coordinator, 25* (1976): 459–464; L. J. Weitzman, "Women and children last: The social and economic consequences of divorce law reforms," in S. M. Dornbusch and M. H. Strober (eds.), *Feminism, children, and the new families* (New York: Guilford Press, 1988), pp. 212–248.

38. J. R. Fleck, C. C. Fuller, S. Z. Malin, D. H. Miller, and K. R. Acheson, "Father psychological absence and heterosexual behavior,

personal adjustment and sex-typing in adolescent girls," *Adolescence, 15* (1980): 847–860.

39. S. Shakur, *Monster: The autobiography of an L.A. gang member* (New York: Penguin Books, 1993); T. Arendell, "After divorce: Investigations into father absence," *Gender and Society, 6* (1992): 562–586.

CHAPTER 2

1. R. D. Parke and B. R. Tinsley, "The father's role in infancy: Determinants of involvement in caregiving and play," in M. E. Lamb (ed.), *The role of the father in child development* (2nd ed.) (New York: Wiley, 1981), pp. 429–458.

2. J. T. Condon, "The assessment of antenatal emotional attachment: Development of a questionnaire instrument," *British Journal of Medical Psychology, 66* (1993): 167–183; C. J. Mebert, "Dimensions of subjectivity in parents' ratings of infant temperament," *Child Development, 62* (1991): 352–361; S. Wolk, C. H. Zeanah, C. T. Garcia-Coll, and S. Carr, "Factors affecting parents' perceptions of temperament in early infancy," *American Journal of Orthopsychiatry, 62* (1992): 71–82.

3. M.D.S. Ainsworth, "Infant-mother attachment," *American Psychologist, 34* (1979): 932–937; J. Bowlby, *Attachment* (New York: Basic Books, 1969).

4. W. A. Collins and M. R. Gunnar, "Social and personality development," *Annual Review of Psychology, 41* (1990): 387–416.

5. M.D.S. Ainsworth, "Attachments beyond infancy," *American Psychologist, 44* (1989): 709–716.

6. N. A. Fox, N. L. Kimmerly, and W. D. Schafer, "Attachment to mother/attachment to father: A meta-analysis," *Child Development, 62* (1991): 210–225.

7. K. S. Bentley and R. A. Fox, "Mothers and fathers of young children: Comparison of parenting styles," *Psychological Reports, 69* (1991): 320–322; D. L. Miller and M. L. Kelley, "Treatment acceptability: The effects of parent gender, marital adjustment, and child behavior," *Child and Family Behavior Therapy, 14* (1992): 11–23.

8. W. A. Collins and G. Russell, "Mother-child and father-child relationships in middle childhood and adolescence: A developmental analysis," *Developmental Review, 11* (1991): 99–136; C. McBride-Chang and C. N. Jacklin, "Early play arousal, sex-typed play, and activity level as precursors to later rough-and-tumble play," *Early Education and Development, 4* (1993): 99–108.

9. M. A. Herman and S. M. McHale, "Coping with parental negativity: Links with parental warmth and child adjustment," *Journal of Applied Developmental Psychology, 14* (1993): 121–130.

10. L. W. Hoffman, "Changes in family roles, socialization, and sex differences," *American Psychologist, 32* (1977): 644–657; N. Radin, "Childrearing fathers in intact families: An exploration of some antecedents and consequences," *Merrill-Palmer Quarterly, 27* (1981): 489–514; N. Radin, "Primary caregiving and role-sharing fathers," in M. E. Lamb (ed.), *Non-traditional families: Parenting and child development* (Hillsdale, NJ: Erlbaum, 1982), pp. 173–204.

11. G. H. Brody, Z. Stoneman, D. Flor, C. McCrary, L. Hastings, and O. Conyers, "Financial resources, parent psychological functioning, parent co-caregiving, and early adolescent competence in rural two-parent African-American families," *Child Development, 65* (1994): 590–605; W. S. Grolnick and M. L. Slowiaczek, "Parents' involvement in children's schooling: A multidimensional conceptualization and motivational model," *Child Development, 65* (1994): 237–252; S. E. Paulson, "Relations of parenting style and parental involvement with ninth-grade students' achievement," *Journal of Early Adolescence, 14* (1994): 250–267; T. E. Smith, "Agreement of adolescent educational expectations with perceived maternal and paternal educational goals," *Youth and Society, 23* (1991): 155–174; A. D. Trice and L. Knapp, "Relationship of children's career aspirations to parents' occupations," *Journal of Genetic Psychology, 153* (1992): 355–357; B. M. Wagner and D. A. Phillips, "Beyond beliefs: Parent and child behaviors and children's perceived academic competence," *Child Development, 63* (1992): 1380–1391; E. Williams and N. Radin, "Paternal involvement, maternal employment, and adolescents' academic achievement: An 11–year follow-up," *American Journal of Orthopsychiatry, 63* (1993): 306–312.

12. P. Bronstein, "Father-child interaction: Implications for gender-role socialization," in P. Bronstein and C. P. Cowan (eds.), *Fatherhood today: Men's changing role in the family* (New York: Wiley, 1988), pp. 107–124; H. Lytton and D. M. Romney, "Parents' differential socialization of boys and girls: A meta-analysis," *Psychological Bulletin, 109* (1991): 267–296; M. Siegal, "Are sons and daughters treated more differently by fathers than by mothers?" *Developmental Review, 7* (1987): 183–209.

13. M. A. Herman and S. M. McHale, "Coping with parental negativity: Links with parental warmth and child adjustment," *Journal of Applied Developmental Psychology, 14* (1993): 121–130; R. Lar-

son, M. Csikszentmihalyi, and R. Graef, "Mood variability and the psychosocial adjustment of adolescents," *Journal of Youth and Adolescence, 9* (1980): 469–490; R. Larson and C. Lampman-Petraitis, "Daily emotional states as reported by children and adolescents," *Child Development, 60* (1989): 1250–1260; D. Offer and K. A. Schonert-Reichl, "Debunking the myths of adolescence: Findings from recent research," *Journal of the American Academy of Child and Adolescent Psychiatry, 31* (1992): 1003–1014.

14. C. M. Buchanan, J. S. Eccles, C. Flanagan, C. Midgley, H. Feldlaufer, and R. D. Harold, "Parents' and teachers' beliefs about adolescents: Effects of sex and experience," *Journal of Youth and Adolescence, 19* (1990): 363–394; M. F. DeLuccie and A. J. Davis, "Father-child relationships from the preschool years through midadolescence," *Journal of Genetic Psychology, 152* (1991): 225–238.

15. S. Bezirganian and P. Cohen, "Sex differences in the interaction between temperament and parenting," *Journal of the American Academy of Child and Adolescent Psychiatry, 31* (1992): 790–801; T. M. McDevitt, R. Lennon, and R. J. Kopriva, "Adolescents' perceptions of mothers' and fathers' prosocial actions and empathic responses," *Youth and Society, 22* (1991): 387–409; D. R. Papini, L. A. Roggman, and J. Anderson, "Early-adolescent perceptions of attachment to mother and father: A test of the emotional-distancing and buffering hypotheses," *Journal of Early Adolescence, 11* (1991): 258–275; S. E. Paulson, J. P. Hill, and G. N. Holmbeck, "Distinguishing between perceived closeness and parental warmth in families with seventh-grade boys and girls," *Journal of Early Adolescence, 11* (1991): 276–293.

16. M. H. Richards, I. B. Gitelson, A. C. Petersen, and A. L. Hurtig, "Adolescent personality in girls and boys," *Psychology of Women Quarterly, 15* (1991): 65–81.

17. J. B. Miller and M. Lane, "Relations between young adults and their parents," *Journal of Adolescence, 14* (1991): 179–194; C. N. Nydegger and L. S. Mitteness, "Fathers and their adult sons and daughters," *Marriage and Family Review, 16* (1991): 249–256; T. S. Parish and J. J. McCluskey, "The relationship between parenting styles and young adults' self-concepts and evaluations of parents," *Adolescence, 27* (1992): 915–918; W. F. Vitulli and B. E. Holland, "College students' attitudes toward relationships with their parents as a function of gender," *Psychological Reports, 72* (1993): 744–746.

18. L. Lawton, M. Silverstein, and V. Bengtson, "Affection, social contact, and geographic distance between adult children and their

parents," *Journal of Marriage and the Family, 56* (1994): 57–68; G. Spitze and J. R. Logan, "Gender differences in family support: Is there a payoff?" *Gerontologist, 29* (1989): 108–113; G. Spitze and S. Miner, "Gender differences in adult child contact among black elderly parents," *Gerontologist, 32* (1992): 213–218.

19. D. Baumrind, "Current patterns of parental authority," *Developmental Psychology Monographs, 4* (1971): 2; E. E. Maccoby, "The role of parents in the socialization of children: An historical overview," *Developmental Psychology, 28* (1992): 1006–1017.

20. L. Anderson, *Dear dad: Letters from an adult child* (New York: Penguin Books, 1989); H. B. Biller and R. J. Trotter, *The father factor: What you need to know to make a difference* (New York: Pocket Books, 1994); B. Cosby, *Fatherhood* (New York: Berkley Books, 1986); W. Glennon, *Fathering: Strengthening connection with your children no matter where you are* (Berkeley, CA: Conari Press, 1995); M. J. Goldman, *The joy of fatherhood: The first twelve months* (Rocklin, CA: Prima Publishing, 1997); B. Greene, *Good morning, Merry Sunshine: A father's journal of his child's first year* (New York: Penguin Books, 1985); R. L. Griswold, *Fatherhood in America: A history* (New York: Basic Books, 1993); E. O. Hutchinson, *Black fatherhood: The guide to male parenting* (Los Angeles: Impact Publications, 1992); J. W. Lindsay, *Teen dads: Rights, responsibilities, and joys* (Buena Park, CA: Morning Glory Press, 1993); C. Marshall, *Expectant father: Helping the father-to-be understand and become a part of the pregnancy experience* (New York: Prima Publishers, 1992); P. Mayle, *How to be a pregnant father* (New York: Carol Publishing Group, 1990); S. Osherson, *The passions of fatherhood* (New York: Fawcett Columbine, 1995); R. D. Parke, *Fatherhood* (Cambridge, MA: Harvard University Press, 1996); J. L. Shapiro, *The measure of a man: Becoming the father you wish your father had been* (New York: Delacorte Press of the Bantam Doubleday Dell Publishing Group, 1993); S. A. Sullivan, *The father's almanac* (rev. ed.) (New York: Doubleday, 1992); A. C. Willis, *Faith of our fathers: African-American men reflect on fatherhood* (New York: Dutton, 1996).

CHAPTER 3

1. P. J. Caplan, *Don't blame mother: Mending the mother-daughter relationship* (New York: Harper and Row, 1989), p. 67; L. B. Silverstein, "Fathering is a feminist issue," *Psychology of Women Quarterly, 20* (1996): 3–37.

2. R. Reed, "Changing conceptions of the maternal instinct," *Journal of Abnormal Psychology and Social Psychology, 18* (1923): 78–87; S. A. Shields, "Functionalism, Darwinism, and the psychology of women: A study of social myth," *American Psychologist, 30* (1975): 739–754; J. B. Watson, "Experimental studies on the growth of the emotions," in M. Bentley, K. Dunlap, W. S. Hunter, K. Koffka, W. Kohler, W. McDougall, M. Prince, J. B. Watson, and R. S. Woodworth (eds.), *Psychologies of 1925* (Worcester, MA: Clark University Press, 1926), pp. 37–57.

3. T. J. Goodrich, "Women, power, and family therapy: What's wrong with this picture?" in T. J. Goodrich (ed.), *Women and power: Perspectives for family therapy* (New York: W. W. Norton, 1991), pp. 3–35; J. Swigart, *The myth of the bad mother: The emotional realities of mothering* (New York: Doubleday, 1991); E. V. Welldon, *Mother, madonna, whore: The idealization and denigration of motherhood* (London: Free Association Books, 1988).

4. R. Reed, "Changing conceptions of the maternal instinct," *Journal of Abnormal Psychology and Social Psychology, 18* (1923): 78–87.

5. J. Bernard, *The future of motherhood* (New York: Dial Press, 1974); J. Bernard, *Women, wives, mothers: Values and options* (Chicago: Aldine Publishing Company, 1975); J. Bernard, *The future of marriage* (New Haven, CT: Yale University Press, 1982); S. Chess, "The 'blame the mother' ideology," *International Journal of Mental Health, 11* (1982): 95–107.

6. G. Bateson, D. D. Jackson, J. Haley, and J. Weakland, "Toward a theory of schizophrenia," *Behavioral Science, 1* (1956): 251–264; F. Fromm-Reichmann, "Notes on the development of treatment of schizophrenics by psychoanalytic psychotherapy," *Psychiatry, 11* (1948): 263–273; M. Mahler, "On child psychosis in schizophrenia: Autistic and symbiotic infantile psychosis," in R. S. Eissler, H. Hartmann, A. Freud, and E. Kris (eds.), *Psychoanalytic study of the child* (Vol. 7) (New York: International University Press, 1952), pp. 286–305; D. J. Miklowitz, A. M. Strachan, M. J. Goldstein, J. A. Doane, K. S. Snyder, G. E. Hogarty, and I.R.H. Falloon, "Expressed emotion and communication deviance in the families of schizophrenics," *Journal of Abnormal Psychology, 95* (1986): 60–66; V. D. Sanua, "The personality and psychological adjustment of family members with autistic children: I. A critical review of the research in Britain," *International Journal of Family Psychiatry, 7* (1986): 221–260; V. D. Sanua, "The personality and psychological adjustment of fam-

ily members of autistic children: II. A critical review of the literature research in the United States," *International Journal of Family Psychiatry, 7* (1986): 331–358.

7. H. F. Harlow, "The nature of love," *American Psychologist, 13* (1958): 673–685.

8. H. F. Harlow, M. K. Harlow, and E. W. Hansen, "The maternal affectional system of rhesus monkeys," in H. L. Rheingold (ed.), *Maternal behavior in mammals* (New York: Wiley, 1963), pp. 254–281.

9. R. Vasta, M. M. Haith, and S. A. Miller, *Child psychology: The modern science,* Vol. 1 (1992): New York: Wiley; E.R.G. Wood, and S. E. Wood, The world of psychology (Needham Heights, MA: Allyn and Bacon, 1996).

10. P. J. Caplan and I. Hall-McCorquodale, "Mother-blaming in major clinical journals," *American Journal of Orthopsychiatry, 55* (1985): 345–353.

11. V. Phares and B. E. Compas, "The role of fathers in child and adolescent psychopathology: Make room for Daddy," *Psychological Bulletin, 111* (1992): 387–412.

12. L. B. Silverstein and V. Phares, "Expanding the parenting paradigm: An examination of dissertation research 1986–1994," *Psychology of Women Quarterly, 20* (1996): 39–53.

13. K. S. Budd and T. P. O'Brien, "Father involvement in behavioral parent training: An area in need of research," *The Behavior Therapist, 5* (1982): 85–89; S. Chess, "Mal de mere," *American Journal of Orthopsychiatry, 34* (1964): 613–614.

14. P. G. Churven, "Families: Parental attitudes to family assessment in a child psychiatry setting," *Journal of Child Psychology and Psychiatry, 19* (1978): 33–41; W. J. Doherty, "Involving the reluctant father in family therapy," in A. S. Gurman (ed.), *Questions and answers in the practice of family therapy* (Vol. 1) (New York: Brunner/Mazel, 1981), pp. 23–26; L. B. Feldman, "Fathers and fathering," in R. L. Meth and R. S. Pasick (eds.), *Men in therapy: The challenge of change* (New York: Guilford Press, 1990), pp. 88–107.

15. T. Gaines, "Engaging the father in family therapy," in A. S. Gurman (ed.), *Questions and answers in the practice of family therapy* (Vol. 1) (New York: Brunner/Mazel, 1981), pp. 20–22; F. W. Kaslow, "Involving the peripheral father in family therapy," in A. S. Gurman (ed.), *Questions and answers in the practice of family therapy* (Vol. 1) (New York: Brunner/Mazel, 1981), pp. 27–31; L. H. Pierce, "Father-son incest: Using the literature to guide practice," *Social Casework, 68*

(1987): 67–74; C. Ringwalt and J. Earp, "Attributing responsibility in cases of father-daughter sexual abuse," *Child Abuse and Neglect, 12* (1988): 273–281; B. Sachs, "Mastering the resistance of working-class fathers to family therapy," *Family Therapy, 13* (1986): 121–132.

16. A. Der-Karabetian and M. Preciado, "Mother-blaming among college students," *Perceptual and Motor Skills, 68* (1989): 453–454.

17. V. Phares, "Perceptions of mothers' and fathers' responsibility for children's behavior," *Sex Roles, 11/12* (1993): 839–851.

18. P. S. Penfold, "Parent's perceived responsibility for children's problems," *Canadian Journal of Psychiatry, 30* (1985): 255–258; J. Watson, "Parental attributions of emotional disturbance and their relation to the outcome of therapy: Preliminary findings," *Australian Psychologist, 21* (1986): 271–282.

19. G. C. Davison and J. M. Neale, *Abnormal psychology* (5th ed.) (New York: Wiley, 1990), p. 396; G. Downey and J. C. Coyne, "Children of depressed parents: An integrative review," *Psychological Bulletin, 108* (1990): 50–76.

20. F. Denmark, N. F. Russo, I. H. Frieze, and J. A. Sechzer, "Guidelines for avoiding sexism in psychological research: A report of the ad hoc committee on nonsexist research," *American Psychologist, 43* (1988): 582–585; E. P. Gama, "Achievement motivation of women: Effects of achievement and affiliation arousal," *Psychology of Women Quarterly, 9* (1985): 89–104; C. Gilligan, *In a different voice* (Cambridge, MA: Harvard University Press, 1982); L. Kohlberg and R. Kramer, "Continuities and discontinuities in childhood and adulthood moral development," *Human Development, 12* (1969): 93–120; D. C. McClelland (ed.), *Studies in motivation* (New York: Appleton-Century-Crofts, 1955); A. Menotti and F. Seccareccia, "Physical activity at work and job responsibility as risk factors for fatal coronary disease and other causes of death," *Journal of Epidemiology and Community Health, 39* (1985): 325–329; C. Patel, "Identifying psychosocial and other risk factors in Whitehall II study," *Homeostasis in Health and Disease, 35* (1994): 71–83; P. Seraganian, E. Roskies, J. A. Hanley, and R. Oseasohn, "Failure to alter psychophysiological reactivity in Type A men with physical exercise or stress management programs," *Psychology and Health, 1* (1987): 195–213.

21. P. J. Caplan, *Don't blame mother: Mending the mother-daughter relationship* (New York: Harper and Row, 1989).

22. S. L. Bem, *The lenses of gender: Transforming the debate on sexual inequality* (New Haven, CT: Yale University Press, 1993); J. Gray, *Men are from Mars, women are from Venus* (New York: Harper Col-

lins, 1992); R. T. Hare-Mustin and J. Marecek (eds.), *Making a difference: Psychology and the construction of gender* (New Haven, CT: Yale University Press, 1990); D. Tannen, *You just don't understand: Women and men in conversation* (New York: Morrow, 1990).

23. Information on gender differences and gender similarities can be found in R. Unger and M. Crawford, *Women and gender: A feminist psychology* (2nd ed.) (New York: McGraw-Hill, 1996).

24. J. Bernard, *Women, wives, mothers: Values and options* (Chicago: Aldine Publishing Company, 1975); P. J. Caplan, *Don't blame mother: Mending the mother-daughter relationship* (New York: Harper and Row, 1989); E. V. Welldon, *Mother, madonna, whore: The idealization and denigration of motherhood* (London: Free Association Books, 1988).

25. J. Bernard, *Women, wives, mothers: Values and options* (Chicago: Aldine Publishing Company, 1975); H. B. Biller and R. J. Trotter, *The father factor: What you need to know to make a difference* (New York: Pocket Books, 1994); P. Chesler, *Women and madness* (New York: Avon Books, 1972).

CHAPTER 4

1. R. Plomin, J. C. DeFries, and G. E. McClearn, *Behavioral genetics: A primer* (2nd ed.) (New York: W. H. Freeman, 1990); J. Dunn and R. Plomin, *Separate lives: Why siblings are so different* (New York: Basic Books, 1990).

2. Unless otherwise noted, all information discussed throughout the book regarding psychiatric diagnoses is based on American Psychiatric Association, *Diagnostic and statistical manual of mental disorders IV* (Washington, DC: American Psychiatric Press, 1994).

3. R. A. Barkley, *Taking charge of AD/HD: The complete authoritative guide for parents* (New York: Guilford Press, 1995); E. M. Hallowell and J. J. Ratey, *Answers to distractions* (New York: Bantam Books, 1994); T. Hartman, *ADD success stories: A guide to fulfillment for families with attention deficit disorder* (Grass Valley, CA: Underwood Books, 1995); B. D. Ingersoll and S. Goldstein, *Attention deficit disorder and learning disabilities: Realities, myths, and controversial treatments* (New York: Doubleday, 1993); R. Kajander, *Living with ADHD: A practical guide to coping with attention deficit hyperactivity disorder* (Minneapolis: Institute for Research and Education Health System in Minnesota, 1995); K. Kelly and P. Ramundo, *You mean I'm not lazy, stupid, or crazy?!: A self-help book for adults with attention deficit disorder* (New York: Scribner, 1995); H. C. Parker, *The ADD hy-*

peractivity workbook for parents, teachers, and kids (2nd ed.) (Plantation, FL: Specialty Press, 1994).

4. R. A. Barkley, Attention deficit hyperactivity disorder: A handbook for diagnosis and treatment (New York: Guilford Press, 1990).

5. J. Alberts-Corush, P. Firestone, and J. T. Goodman, "Attention and impulsivity characteristics of the biological and adoptive parents of hyperactive and normal control children," American Journal of Orthopsychiatry, 56 (1986): 413–423; C. E. Cunningham, B. B. Benness, and L. S. Siegel, "Family functioning, time allocation, and parental depression in the families of normal and ADDH children," Journal of Clinical Child Psychology, 17 (1988): 169–177; E. J. Mash and C. Johnston, "Parental perceptions of child behavior problems, parenting self-esteem, and mothers' reported stress in younger and older hyperactive and normal children," Journal of Consulting and Clinical Psychology, 51 (1983): 86–99; J. C. Reeves, J. S. Werry, G. S. Elkind, and A. Zametkin, "Attention deficit, conduct, oppositional, and anxiety disorders in children: II. Clinical characteristics," Journal of the American Academy of Child and Adolescent Psychiatry, 26 (1987): 144–155; M. P. Sobol, D. T. Ashbourne, B. M. Earn, and C. E. Cunningham, "Parents' attributions for achieving compliance from attention-deficit disordered children," Journal of Abnormal Child Psychology, 17 (1989): 359–369.

6. C. E. Cunningham et al., "Family functioning, time allocation, and parental depression in the families of normal and ADDH children," Journal of Clinical Child Psychology, 17 (1988): 169–177; A. R. Lang, W. E. Pelham, C. Johnston, and S. Gelernter, "Levels of adult alcohol consumption induced by interactions with child confederates exhibiting normal versus externalizing behaviors," Journal of Abnormal Psychology, 98 (1989): 294–299.

7. P. J. Frick, B. B. Lahey, M.A.G. Christ, R. Loeber, and S. Green, "History of childhood behavior problems in biological relatives of boys with attention-deficit hyperactivity disorder and conduct disorder," Journal of Clinical Child Psychology, 20 (1991): 445–451.

8. J. Alberts-Corush et al., "Attention and impulsivity characteristics of the biological and adoptive parents of hyperactive and normal control children," American Journal of Orthopsychiatry, 56 (1986): 413–423; C. E. Cunningham et al., "Family functioning, time allocation, and parental depression in the families of normal and ADDH children," Journal of Clinical Child Psychology, 17 (1988): 169–177; R. Goodman and J. Stevenson, "A twin study of hyperactivity: II. The

aetiological role of genes, family relationships and perinatal adversity," *Journal of Child Psychology and Psychiatry, 30* (1989): 691–709.

9. D. B. Baker, "Parenting stress and ADHD: A comparison of mothers and fathers," *Journal of Emotional and Behavioral Disorders, 2* (1994): 46–50; C. E. Cunningham et al., "Family functioning, time allocation, and parental depression in the families of normal and ADDH children," *Journal of Clinical Child Psychology, 17* (1988): 169–177.

10. R. A. Barkley, *Taking charge of AD/HD: The complete authoritative guide for parents* (New York: Guilford Press, 1995).

11. J. F. Alexander, H. B. Waldron, C. Barton, and C. H. Mas, "The minimizing of blaming attributions and behaviors in delinquent families," *Journal of Consulting and Clinical Psychology, 57* (1989): 19–24; R. Atwood, M. Gold, and R. Taylor, "Two types of delinquents and their institutional adjustment," *Journal of Consulting and Clinical Psychology, 57* (1989): 68–75; C. M. Borduin, J. A. Pruitt, and S. W. Henggeler, "Family interactions in black, lower-class families with delinquent and nondelinquent adolescent boys," *Journal of Genetic Psychology, 147* (1986): 333–342; P. J. Frick et al., "History of childhood behavior problems in biological relatives of boys with attention-deficit hyperactivity disorder and conduct disorder," *Journal of Clinical Child Psychology, 20* (1991): 445–451; A. Goetting, "The parenting-crime connection," *Journal of Primary Prevention, 14* (1994): 169–186; M. L. Jary and M. A. Stewart, "Psychiatric disorder in the parents of adopted children with aggressive conduct disorder," *Neuropsychobiology, 13* (1985): 7–11; B. B. Lahey, J. C. Piacentini, K. McBurnett, P. Stone, S. Hartdagen, and G. Hynd, "Psychopathology in the parents of children with conduct disorder and hyperactivity," *Journal of the American Academy of Child and Adolescent Psychiatry, 27* (1988): 163–170; R. Loeber, "Development and risk factors of juvenile antisocial behavior and delinquency," *Clinical Psychology Review, 10* (1990): 1–41; R. Loeber and T. J. Dishion, "Antisocial and delinquent youths: Methods for their early identification," in J. D. Burchard and S. N. Burchard (eds.), *Prevention of delinquent behavior* (Newbury Park, CA: Sage, 1987), pp. 75–89; J. C. Reeves et al., "Attention deficit, conduct, oppositional, and anxiety disorders in children: II. Clinical characteristics," *Journal of the American Academy of Child and Adolescent Psychiatry, 26* (1987): 144–155; R. Schachar and R. Wachsmuth, "Oppositional disorder in children: A validation study comparing conduct disorder, oppositional disorder and normal

control children," *Journal of Child Psychology and Psychiatry, 31* (1990): 1089–1102.

12. K. M. Heide, *Why kids kill parents: Child abuse and adolescent homicide* (Columbus, OH: Ohio State University Press, 1992); D. O. Lewis, J. H. Pincus, R. Lovely, E. Spitzer, and E. Moy, "Biopsychosocial characteristics of matched samples of delinquents and nondelinquents," *Journal of the American Academy of Child and Adolescent Psychiatry, 26* (1987): 744–752; D. O. Lewis, S. S. Shanok, M. Grant, and E. Ritvo, "Homicidally aggressive young children: Neuropsychiatric and experiential correlates," *American Journal of Psychiatry, 140* (1983): 148–153; D. Lisak, "Sexual aggression, masculinity, and fathers," *Signs: Journal of Women in Culture and Society, 16* (1991): 238–262; D. Lisak and S. Roth, "Motives and psychodynamics of self-reported, unincarcerated rapists," *American Journal of Orthopsychiatry, 60* (1990): 268–280; S. Singhal and A. Dutta, "Who commits patricide?" *Acta Psychiatrica Scandinavica, 82* (1990): 40–43; D. Truscott, "Intergenerational transmission of violent behavior in adolescent males," *Aggressive Behavior, 18* (1992): 327–335; J. K. Warren, F. Gary, and J. Moorhead, "Self-reported experiences of physical and sexual abuse among runaway youths," *Perspectives in Psychiatric Care, 30* (1994): 23–28.

13. G. Hamdan-Allen, M. A. Stewart, and J. H. Beeghly, "Subgrouping conduct disorder by psychiatric family history," *Journal of Child Psychology and Psychiatry, 30* (1989): 889–897; B. B. Lahey et al., "Psychopathology in the parents of children with conduct disorder and hyperactivity," *Journal of the American Academy of Child and Adolescent Psychiatry, 27* (1988): 163–170; R. Loeber and M. Stouthamer-Loeber, "Family factors as correlates and predictors of juvenile conduct problems and delinquency," in M. Tonry and N. Morris (eds.), *Crime and Justice* (Vol. 7) (Chicago: University of Chicago Press, 1986), pp. 219–339; F. Rothbaum and J. R. Weisz, "Parental caregiving and child externalizing behavior in nonclinical samples: A meta-analysis," *Psychological Bulletin, 116* (1994): 55–74; M. M. Vanyukov, H. B. Moss, J. A. Plail, and T. Blackson, "Antisocial symptoms in preadolescent boys and in their parents: Associations with cortisol," *Psychiatry Research, 46* (1993): 9–17.

14. S. W. Henggeler, J. Edwards, and C. M. Borduin, "The family relations of female juvenile delinquents," *Journal of Abnormal Child Psychology, 15* (1987): 199–209; P. L. Johnson and K. D. O'Leary, "Parental behavior patterns and conduct disorders in girls," *Journal of Abnormal Child Psychology, 15* (1987): 573–581; K. Kavanagh and H.

Hops, "Good girls? Bad boys? Gender and development as contexts for diagnosis and treatment," in T. H. Ollendick and R. J. Prinz (eds.), *Advances in clinical child psychology* (Vol. 16) (New York: Plenum, 1994), pp. 45–79.

15. M. D. Free, "Clarifying the relationship between the broken home and juvenile delinquency: A critique of the current literature," *Deviant Behavior: An Interdisciplinary Journal, 12* (1991): 109–167; R. Loeber, "Development and risk factors of juvenile antisocial behavior and delinquency," *Clinical Psychology Review, 10* (1990): 1–41; H. Yoshikawa, "Prevention as cumulative protection: Effects of early family support and education on chronic delinquency and its risks," *Psychological Bulletin, 115* (1994): 28–54.

16. C. R. Brewin, R. Andrews, and I. H. Gotlib, "Psychopathology and early experience: A reappraisal of retrospective reports," *Psychological Bulletin, 113* (1993): 82–98; C.A.J. DeJong, F. M. Harteveld, and G.E.M. van de Wielen, "Memories of parental rearing in alcohol and drug addicts: A comparative study," *International Journal of the Addictions, 26* (1991): 1065–1076; K. S. Kendler, J. L. Silberg, M. C. Neale, R. C. Kessler, A. C. Heath, and L. Eaves, "The family history method: Whose psychiatric history is measured?" *American Journal of Psychiatry, 148* (1991): 1501–1504.

17. J. D. Hawkins, R. F. Catalano, and J. Y. Miller, "Risk and protective factors for alcohol and other drug problems in adolescence and early adulthood: Implications for substance abuse prevention," *Psychological Bulletin, 112* (1992): 64–105; Z. Hrubec, and G. S. Omenn, "Evidence of genetic predisposition to alcoholic cirrhosis and psychosis: Twin concordances for alcoholism and its biological end points by zygosity among male veterans," *Alcoholism, 5* (1981): 207–215; V. E. Pollock, L. S. Schneider, W. F. Gabrielli, and D. W. Goodwin, "Sex of parent and offspring in the transmission of alcoholism: A meta-analysis," *Journal of Nervous and Mental Disease, 175* (1987): 668–673.

18. A. C. Petersen, B. E. Compas, J. Brooks-Gunn, M. Stemmler, S. Ey, and K. E. Grant, "Depression in adolescence," *American Psychologist, 48* (1993): 155–168.

19. D. A. Cole, and L. P. Rehm, "Family interaction patterns and childhood depression," *Journal of Abnormal Child Psychology, 14* (1986): 297–314; H. Hops, "Parental depression and child behavior problems: Implications for behavioural family intervention," *Behaviour Change, 9* (1992): 126–138; P. S. Jensen, L. Bloedau, J. Degroot, T. Ussery, and H. Davis, "Children at risk: I. Risk factors and child

symptomatology," *Journal of the American Academy of Child and Adolescent Psychiatry, 29* (1990): 51–59; N. J. Kaslow, L. P. Rehm, S. L. Pollack, and A. W. Siegel, "Attributional style and self-control behavior in depressed and nondepressed children and their parents," *Journal of Abnormal Child Psychology, 16* (1988): 163–175; R. A. Weller, P. Kapadia, E. B. Weller, M. Fristad, L. B. Lazaroff, and S. H. Preskorn, "Psychopathology in families of children with major depressive disorders," *Journal of Affective Disorders, 31* (1994): 247–252.

20. D. A. Cole and A. E. McPherson, "Relation of family subsystems to adolescent depression: Implementing a new family assessment strategy," *Journal of Family Psychology, 7* (1993): 119–133; K. John, G. D. Gammon, B. A. Prusoff, and V. Warner, "The Social Adjustment Inventory for Children and Adolescents (SAICA): Testing of a new semistructured interview," *Journal of the American Academy of Child and Adolescent Psychiatry, 26* (1987): 898–911; J. Puig-Antich, J. Kaufman, N. D. Ryan, and D. E. Williamson, "The psychosocial functioning and family environment of depressed adolescents," *Journal of the American Academy of Child and Adolescent Psychiatry, 32* (1993): 244–253.

21. C. Gerlsma, P.M.G. Emmelkamp, and W. A. Arrindell, "Anxiety, depression, and perception of early parenting: A meta-analysis," *Clinical Psychology Review, 10* (1990): 251–277; K. S. Kendler et al., "The family history method: Whose psychiatric history is measured?" *American Journal of Psychiatry, 148* (1991): 1501–1504.

22. D. A. Clark and D. Bolton, "Obsessive-compulsive adolescents and their parents: A psychometric study," *Journal of Child Psychology and Psychiatry, 26* (1985): 267–276; C. G. Last and C. C. Strauss, "Panic disorder in children and adolescents," *Journal of Anxiety Disorders, 3* (1989): 87–95; M. C. Lenane, S. E. Swedo, H. Leonard, D. L. Pauls, W. Sceery, and J. L. Rapoport, "Psychiatric disorders in first degree relatives of children and adolescents with obsessive compulsive disorder," *Journal of the American Academy of Child and Adolescent Psychiatry, 29* (1990): 407–412; J. C. Reeves et al., "Attention deficit, conduct, oppositional, and anxiety disorders in children: II. Clinical characteristics," *Journal of the American Academy of Child and Adolescent Psychiatry, 26* (1987): 144–155.

23. M. C. Angermeyer, "The association between family atmosphere and hospital career of schizophrenic patients," *British Journal of Psychiatry, 141* (1982): 1–11; J. Dunn and R. Plomin, *Separate lives: Why siblings are so different* (New York: Basic Books, 1990); K. Hahlweg, M. J. Goldstein, K. H. Nuechterlein, A. B. Magana, J. Mintz, J.

A. Doane, D. J. Miklowitz, and K. S. Snyder, "Expressed emotion and patient-relative interaction in families of recent onset schizophrenics," *Journal of Consulting and Clinical Psychology*, 57 (1989): 11–18; D. J. Miklowitz, M. J. Goldstein, J. A. Doane, K. H. Nuechterlein, A. M. Strachan, K. S. Snyder, and A. Magana-Amato, "Is expressed emotion an index of a transactional process? I. Parents' affective style," *Family Process*, 28 (1989): 153–167; S. Onstad, I. Skre, S. Torgersen, and E. Kringlen, "Parental representation in twins discordant for schizophrenia," *Psychological Medicine*, 23 (1993): 335–340; A. M. Strachan, D. Feingold, M. J. Goldstein, D. J. Miklowitz, and K. H. Nuechterlein, "Is expressed emotion an index of a transactional process? II. Patient's coping style," *Family Process*, 28 (1989): 169–181; J. A. Yesavage, J.M.T. Becker, P. D. Werner, M. J. Patton, K. Seeman, D. W. Brunsting, and M. J. Mills, "Family conflict, psychopathology, and dangerous behavior by schizophrenic inpatients," *Psychiatry Research*, 8 (1983): 271–280.

24. N. L. Freeman, A. Perry, and D. C. Factor, "Child behaviours as stressors: Replicating and extending the use of the CARS as a measure of stress: A research note," *Journal of Clinical Psychology and Psychiatry*, 32 (1991): 1025–1030; D. Moes, R. L. Koegel, L. Schreibman, and L. M. Loos, "Stress profiles for mothers and fathers of children with autism," *Psychological Reports*, 71 (1992): 1272–1274; V. D. Sanua, "The personality and psychological adjustment of family members with autistic children: I. A critical review of the research in Britain," *International Journal of Family Psychiatry*, 7 (1986): 221–260; V. D. Sanua, "The personality and psychological adjustment of family members of autistic children: II. A critical review of the literature research in the United States," *International Journal of Family Psychiatry*, 7 (1986): 331–358.

25. J. Rodin, L. F. Silberstein, and R. H. Striegel-Moore, "Women and weight: A normative discontent," in T. B. Sonderegger (ed.), *Psychology and gender: Nebraska symposium on motivation* (Lincoln: University of Nebraska Press, 1985), pp. 267–307; J. K. Thompson, *Body image, eating disorders, and obesity* (Washington, DC: American Psychological Association, 1996).

26. R. Calam, G. Waller, P. D. Slade, and T. Newton, "Eating disorders and perceived relationships with parents," *International Journal of Eating Disorders*, 9 (1990): 479–485; L. L. Humphrey, "Observed family interactions among subtypes of eating disorders using structural analysis of social behavior," *Journal of Consulting and Clinical Psychology*, 57 (1989): 206–214; K. S. Kendler, C. MacLean,

M. C. Neale, R. C. Kessler, A. C. Heath, and L. Eaves, "The genetic epidemiology of bulimia nervosa," *American Journal of Psychiatry, 148* (1991): 1627–1637; A. Russell, G. Russell, and D. Midwinter, "Observer influences on mothers and fathers: Self-reported influence during a home observation," *Merrill-Palmer Quarterly, 38* (1992): 263–283; A. Telerant, J. Kronenberg, S. Rabinovitch, and I. Elman, "Anorectic family dynamics," *Journal of the American Academy of Child and Adolescent Psychiatry, 31* (1992): 990–991.

27. R. F. Eme, and M. H. Danielak, "Comparison of fathers of daughters with and without maladaptive eating attitudes," *Journal of Emotional and Behavioral Disorders, 3* (1995): 40–45.

28. M. Maine, *Father hunger: Fathers, daughters and food* (Carlsbad, CA: Gurze Books, 1991).

CHAPTER 5

1. E. E. Werner, "Resilience in development," *Current Directions in Psychological Science, 4* (1995): 81–85.

2. E. Kandel, S. A. Mednick, L. Kirkegaard-Sorensen, B. Hutchings, J. Knop, R. Rosenberg, and F. Schulsinger, "IQ as a protective factor for subjects at high risk for antisocial behavior," *Journal of Consulting and Clinical Psychology, 56* (1988): 224–226.

3. C. S. Lanier, "Dimensions of father-child interaction in a New York state prison population," *Journal of Offender Rehabilitation, 16* (1991): 27–42.

4. C. F. Hairston, "Men in prisons: Family characteristics and parenting views," *Journal of Offender Counseling, Services and Rehabilitation, 14* (1989): 23–30.

5. A. Berkowitz and H. W. Perkins, "Personality characteristics of children of alcoholics," *Journal of Consulting and Clinical Psychology, 56* (1988): 206–209; T. A. Cavell, D. C. Jones, R. D. Runyan, and L. P. Constantin-Page, "Perceptions of attachment and the adjustment of adolescents with alcoholic fathers," *Journal of Family Psychology, 7* (1993): 204–212; L. E. Dumka and M. W. Roosa, "Factors mediating problem drinking and mothers' personal adjustment," *Journal of Family Psychology, 7* (1993): 333–343; H. E. Fitzgerald, L. A. Sullivan, H. P. Ham, and R. A. Zucker, "Predictors of behavior problems in three-year-old sons of alcoholics: Early evidence for the onset of risk," *Child Development, 64* (1993): 110–123; E. Maguin, R. A. Zucker, and H. E. Fitzgerald, "The path to alcohol problems through conduct problems: A family based approach to early intervention

with risk," *Journal of Research on Adolescence*, 4 (1994): 249–269; R. A. Seilhamer, T. Jacob, and N. J. Dunn, "The impact of alcohol consumption on parent-child relationships in families of alcoholics," *Journal of Studies on Alcohol*, 54 (1993): 189–198; R. E. Tarter, T. C. Blackson, C. S. Martin, and R. Loeber, "Characteristics and correlates of child discipline practices in substance abuse and normal families," *American Journal on Addictions*, 2 (1993): 18–25; N. Z. Weinberg, T. E. Dielman, W. Mandell, and J. T. Shope, "Parental drinking and gender factors in the prediction of early adolescent alcohol use," *International Journal of the Addictions*, 29 (1994): 89–104; M. O. West and R. J. Prinz, "Parental alcoholism and childhood psychopathology," *Psychological Bulletin*, 102 (1987): 204–218; S. C. Whipple and E. P. Noble, "Personality characteristics of alcoholic fathers and their sons," *Journal of Studies on Alcohol*, 52 (1991): 331–337.

6. J. A. deLong and A. Roy, "Paternal lineage of alcoholism, cohort effects, and alcoholism criteria," *Addiction*, 88 (1993): 623–629; J. D. Hawkins, R. F. Catalano, and J. Y. Miller, "Risk and protective factors for alcohol and other drug problems in adolescence and early adulthood: Implications for substance abuse prevention," *Psychological Bulletin*, 112 (1992): 64–105; R. O. Pihl, J. Peterson, and P. R. Finn, "Inherited predisposition to alcoholism: Characteristics of sons of male alcoholics," *Journal of Abnormal Psychology*, 99 (1990): 291–301.

7. R. T. Murphy, T. J. O'Farrell, F. J. Floyd, and G. J. Connors, "School adjustment of children of alcoholic fathers: Comparison to normal controls," *Addictive Behaviors*, 16 (1991): 275–287; R. E. Tarter, A. M. Hegedus, and J. S. Gavaler, "Hyperactivity in sons of alcoholics," *Journal of Studies on Alcohol*, 46 (1985): 259–261; R. E. Tarter, A. M. Hegedus, G. Goldstein, C. Shelly, and A. I. Alterman, "Adolescent sons of alcoholics: Neuropsychological and personality characteristics," *Alcoholism: Clinical and Experimental Research*, 8 (1984): 216–222.

8. N. el-Guebaly, D. R. Offord, K. T. Sullivan, and G. W. Lynch, "Psychosocial adjustment of the offspring of psychiatric inpatients: The effect of alcoholic, depressive and schizophrenic parentage," *Canadian Psychiatric Association Journal*, 23 (1978): 281–289; T. Jacob, G. L. Krahn, and K. Leonard, "Parent-child interactions in families with alcoholic fathers," *Journal of Consulting and Clinical Psychology*, 59 (1991): 176–181.

9. A. L. Jarmas and A. E. Kazak, "Young adult children of alcoholic fathers: Depressive experiences, coping styles, and family sys-

tems," *Journal of Consulting and Clinical Psychology, 60* (1992): 244–251; K. J. Sher, *Children of alcoholics: A critical appraisal of theory and research* (Chicago: University of Chicago Press, 1991); K. J. Sher, K. S. Walitzer, P. K. Wood, and E. E. Brent, "Characteristics of children of alcoholics: Putative risk factors, substance use and abuse, and psychopathology," *Journal of Abnormal Psychology, 100* (1991): 427–448; R. Velleman, "Intergenerational effects—A review of environmentally oriented studies concerning the relationship between parental alcohol problems and family disharmony in the genesis of alcohol and other problems: I. The intergenerational effects of alcohol problems," *International Journal of the Addictions, 27* (1992): 253–280.

10. K. S. Kendler, M. C. Neale, A. C. Heath, and R. C. Kessler, "A twin-family study of alcoholism in women," *American Journal of Psychiatry, 151* (1994): 707–715; M. A. Schuckit, J. E. Tipp, and E. Kelner, "Are daughters of alcoholics more likely to marry alcoholics?" *American Journal of Drug and Alcohol Abuse, 20* (1994): 237–245.

11. C. T. Giunta and B. E. Compas, "Adult daughters of alcoholics: Are they unique?" *Journal of Studies on Alcohol, 55* (1994): 600–606.

12. G. Downey and J. C. Coyne, "Children of depressed parents: An integrative review," *Psychological Bulletin, 108* (1990): 50–76; N. J. Kaslow, C. G. Deering, and G. R. Racusin, "Depressed children and their families," *Clinical Psychology Review, 14* (1994): 39–59; A. C. Petersen, B. E. Compas, J. Brooks-Gunn, and M. Stemmler, "Depression in adolescence," *American Psychologist, 48* (1993): 155–168.

13. W. R. Beardslee, L. H. Schultz, and R. L. Selman, "Level of social-cognitive development, adaptive functioning, and DSM-III diagnoses in adolescent offspring of parents with affective disorders: Implications of the development of the capacity for mutuality," *Developmental Psychology, 23* (1987): 807–815; A. Harjan, "Children of parents with affective disorders: The role of an ill mother or an ill father," *European Journal of Psychiatry, 6* (1992): 74–87; T. Jacob and K. Leonard, "Psychosocial functioning in children of alcoholic fathers, depressed fathers and control fathers," *Journal of Studies on Alcohol, 47* (1986): 373–380; H. Orvaschel, G. Walsh-Allis, and W. Ye, "Psychopathology in children of parents with recurrent depression," *Journal of Abnormal Child Psychology, 16* (1988): 17–28; A. M. Thomas and R. Forehand, "The relationship between paternal depressive mood and early adolescent functioning," *Journal of Family Psychology, 4* (1991): 260–271.

14. A. K. Atkinson and A. U. Rickel, "Postpartum depression in primiparous parents," *Journal of Abnormal Psychology, 93* (1984): 115–119; M. G. Carro, K. E. Grant, I. H. Gotlib, and B. E. Compas, "Postpartum depression and child development: An investigation of mothers and fathers as sources of risk and resilience," *Development and Psychopathology, 5* (1993): 567–579.

15. G. Downey and J. C. Coyne, "Children of depressed parents: An integrative review," *Psychological Bulletin, 108* (1990): 50–76.

16. M. Conrad and C. Hammen, "Protective and resource factors in high- and low-risk children: A comparison of children with unipolar, bipolar, medically ill, and normal mothers," *Development and Psychopathology, 5* (1993): 593–607; H. Hops, A. Biglan, L. Sherman, J. Arthur, L. Friedman, and V. Osteen, "Home observations of family interactions of depressed women," *Journal of Consulting and Clinical Psychology, 55* (1987): 341–346; L. Tannenbaum and R. Forehand, *Maternal depressed mood and adolescent functioning: Fathers do make a difference* (poster presented at the convention of the Association for the Advancement of Behavior Therapy, Atlanta, GA, November 1993).

17. M. M. Weissman, E. S. Gershon, K. K. Kidd, B. A. Prusoff, J. F. Leckman, E. Dibble, J. Hamovit, D. Thompson, D. L. Pauls, and J. J. Guroff, "Psychiatric disorders in the relatives of probands with affective disorders," *Archives of General Psychiatry, 41* (1984): 13–21.

18. K. Deater-Deckard, S. Scarr, K. McCartney, and M. Eisenberg, "Paternal separation anxiety: Relationships with parenting stress, child-rearing attitudes, and maternal anxieties," *Psychological Science, 5* (1994): 341–346.

19. B. K. Jordan, C. R. Marmar, J. A. Fairbank, W. E. Schlenger, R. A. Kulka, R. L. Hough, and D. S. Weiss, "Problems in families of male Vietnam veterans with posttraumatic stress disorder," *Journal of Consulting and Clinical Psychology, 60* (1992): 916–926; J. Parsons, T. J. Kehle, and S. V. Owen, "Incidence of behavior problems among children of Vietnam War veterans," *School Psychology International, 11* (1990): 253–259; R. Rosenheck, "Impact of posttraumatic stress disorder of World War II on the next generation," *Journal of Nervous and Mental Disease, 174* (1986): 319–327.

20. S. M. Turner, D. C. Beidel, and A. Costello, "Psychopathology in the offspring of anxiety disorders patients," *Journal of Consulting and Clinical Psychology, 55* (1987): 229–235.

21. J. H. Coverdale, D. Schotte, P. Ruiz, S. Pharies, and T. Bayer, "Family planning needs of male chronic mental patients in the gen-

eral hospital psychiatry clinic," *General Hospital Psychiatry, 16* (1994): 38–41; J. Dunn and R. Plomin, *Separate lives: Why siblings are so different* (New York: Basic Books (1990); K. R. Merikangas, B. A. Prusoff, and M. M. Weissman, "Parental concordance for affective disorders: Psychopathology in offspring," *Journal of Affective Disorders, 15* (1988): 279–290; N. F. Watt, "Risk research in schizophrenia and other major psychological disorders," in M. Kessler and S. E. Goldston (eds.), *A decade of progress in primary prevention* (Hanover, NH: University of Press of New England, 1986), pp. 115–153.

22. J. Rolf, A. S. Masten, D. Cicchetti, K. H. Neuchterlein, and S. Weintraub (eds.), *Risk and protective factors in the development of psychopathology* (New York: Cambridge University Press, 1990); N. F. Watt, E. J. Anthony, L. C. Wynne, and J. E. Rolf (eds.), *Children at risk for schizophrenia: A longitudinal perspective* (New York: Cambridge University Press, 1984).

23. E. W. Holden and G. A. Banez, "Child abuse potential and parenting stress within maltreating families," *Journal of Family Violence, 11* (1996): 1–12; C. Wekerle and D. A. Wolfe, "Child maltreatment," in E. J. Mash and R. A. Barkley (eds.), *Child psychopathology* (New York: Guilford Press, 1996), pp. 492–537; D. A. Wolfe, "Child-abusive parents: An empirical review and analysis," *Psychological Bulletin, 97* (1985): 462–482.

24. J. Kaufman and E. Zigler, "The intergenerational transmission of child abuse and the prospect of predicting future abusers," in D. Cicchetti and V. Carlson (eds.), *Child maltreatment: Research and theory on the causes and consequences of child abuse and neglect* (New York: Cambridge University Press, 1989), pp. 129–150; C. Wekerle and D. A. Wolfe, "Child maltreatment," in E. J. Mash and R. A. Barkley (eds.), *Child psychopathology* (New York: Guilford Press, 1996), pp. 492–537.

25. G. D. Wolfner and R. J. Gelles, "A profile of violence toward children: A national study," *Child Abuse and Neglect, 17* (1993): 197–212.

26. A. Diacatou, G. Mamalakis, A. Kafatos, and J. Vlahonikolis, "Alcohol, tobacco, and father's aggressive behavior in relation to socioeconomic variables in Cretan low versus medium income families," *International Journal of the Addictions, 28* (1993): 293–304; J. B. Reid, K. Kavanagh, and D. V. Baldwin, "Abusive parents' perceptions of child problem behaviors: An example of parental bias," *Journal of Abnormal Child Psychology, 15* (1987): 457–466; E. E. Whipple

and C. Webster-Stratton, "The role of parental stress in physically abusive families," *Child Abuse and Neglect, 15* (1991): 279–291.

27. M. O'Keefe, "Linking marital violence, mother-child/father-child aggression, and child behavior problems," *Journal of Family Violence, 9* (1994): 63–78; K. J. Sternberg, M. E. Lamb, C. Greenbaum, D. Cicchetti, S. Dawud, R. M. Cortes, O. Krispin, and F. Lorey, "Effects of domestic violence on children's behavior problems and depression," *Developmental Psychology, 29* (1993): 44–52.

28. J. H. Beitchman, K. J. Zucker, J. E. Hood, G. A. DaCosta, D. Akman, and E. Cassavia, "A review of the long-term effects of child sexual abuse," *Child Abuse and Neglect, 16* (1992): 101–118; D. Finkelhor, "Early and long-term effects of child sexual abuse: An update," *Professional Psychology: Research and Practice, 21* (1990): 325–330; J. Herman and L. Hirschman, "Families at risk for father-daughter incest," *American Journal of Psychiatry, 138* (1981): 967–971; M. Hunter, *Abused boys: The neglected victims of sexual abuse* (New York: Fawcett, 1990); S. V. McLeer, E. B. Deblinger, D. Henry, and H. Orvaschel, "Sexually abused children at high risk for post-traumatic stress disorder," *Journal of the American Academy of Child and Adolescent Psychiatry, 31* (1992): 875–879.

29. E. Bass and L. Davis, *The courage to heal: A guide for women survivors of child sexual abuse* (3rd ed.) (New York: HarperCollins, 1994); J. Bigras, P. Leichner, M. Perreault, and R. Lavoie, "Severe paternal sexual abuse in early childhood and systematic aggression against the family and the institution," *Canadian Journal of Psychiatry, 36* (1991): 527–529; E. Deblinger, C. R. Hathaway, J. Lippmann, and R. Steer, "Psychosocial characteristics and correlates of symptom distress in nonoffending mothers of sexually abused children," *Journal of Interpersonal Violence, 8* (1993): 155–168; M. Hunter (ed.), *Adult survivors of sexual abuse: Treatment innovations* (Thousand Oaks, CA: Sage, 1995); T. J. Reidy and N. J. Hochstadt, "Attribution of blame in incest cases: A comparison of mental health professionals," *Child Abuse and Neglect, 17* (1993): 371–381; C. Ringwalt and J. Earp, "Attributing responsibility in cases of father-daughter sexual abuse," *Child Abuse and Neglect, 12* (1988): 273–281.

30. H. Parker and S. Parker, "Father-daughter sexual abuse: An emerging perspective," *American Journal of Orthopsychiatry, 56* (1986): 531–549.

31. G. Albee, S. Gordon, and H. Leitenberg (eds.), *Promoting sexual responsibility and preventing sexual problems* (Hanover, NH: University Press of New England, 1983); D. A. Daro, "Prevention of

child sexual abuse," *The Future of Children*, *4* (1994): 198–223; D. Finkelhor and N. Strapko, "Sexual abuse prevention education: A review of evaluation studies," in D. J. Willis, E. W. Holden, and M. Rosenberg (eds.), *Prevention of child maltreatment: Developmental and ecological perspectives* (New York: Wiley, 1992).

CHAPTER 6

1. Consumer Reports, "Mental health: Does therapy work?" *Consumer Reports* (November 1995): 734–739.

2. D. S. Becvar and R. J. Becvar, *Family therapy: A systemic integration* (2nd ed.) (Needham Heights, MA: Allyn and Bacon, 1993); M. D. Hazelrigg, H. M. Cooper, and C. M. Borduin, "Evaluating the effectiveness of family therapies: An integrative review and analysis," *Psychological Bulletin*, *101* (1987): 428–442; E. D. Hibbs and P. S. Jensen (eds.), *Psychosocial treatments for child and adolescent disorders: Empirically based strategies for clinical practice* (Washington, DC: American Psychological Association, 1996); A. E. Kazdin, "Effectiveness of psychotherapy with children and adolescents," *Journal of Consulting and Clinical Psychology*, *59* (1991): 785–798; J. R. Weisz, B. Weiss, S. S. Han, and D. A. Granger, "Effects of psychotherapy with children and adolescents revisited: A meta-analysis of treatment outcome studies," *Psychological Bulletin*, *117* (1995): 450–468.

3. R. A. Barkley, *Attention deficit hyperactivity disorder: A handbook for diagnosis and treatment* (New York: Guilford Press, 1990); E. D. Hibbs and P. S. Jensen (eds.), *Psychosocial treatments for child and adolescent disorders: Empirically based strategies for clinical practice* (Washington, DC: American Psychological Association, 1996).

4. R. A. Barkley, *Defiant children: A clinician's manual for parent training* (New York: Guilford Press, 1987).

5. V. J. Adesso and J. W. Lipson, "Group training of parents as therapists for their children," *Behavior Therapy*, *12* (1981): 625–633; P. Firestone, M. J. Kelly, and S. Fike, "Are fathers necessary in parent training groups?" *Journal of Clinical Child Psychology*, *9* (1980): 44–47; B. Martin, "Brief family intervention: Effectiveness and the importance of including the father," *Journal of Consulting and Clinical Psychology*, *45* (1977): 1002–1010; J. J. Reisinger, "Unprogrammed learning of differential attention by fathers of oppositional children," *Journal of Behavior Therapy and Experimental Psychiatry*, *13* (1982): 203–208; C. Webster-Stratton, "The effects of father involvement in parent training for conduct problem children," *Journal of Child Psy-*

chology and Psychiatry, 26 (1985): 801–810; C. Webster-Stratton, "Individually administered videotape parent training: Who benefits?" *Cognitive Therapy and Research, 16* (1992): 31–35; C. Webster-Stratton, T. Hollinsworth, and M. Kolpacoff, "The long-term effectiveness and clinical significance of three cost-effective training programs for families with conduct-problem children," *Journal of Consulting and Clinical Psychology, 57* (1989): 550–553; C. Webster-Stratton, M. Kolpacoff, and T. Hollinsworth, "Self-administered videotape therapy for families with conduct-problem children: Comparison with two cost-effective treatments and a control group," *Journal of Consulting and Clinical Psychology, 56* (1988): 558–566.

6. J. F. Alexander, H. B. Waldron, C. Barton, and C. H. Mas, "The minimizing of blaming attributions and behaviors in delinquent families," *Journal of Consulting and Clinical Psychology, 57* (1989): 19–24; S. W. Henggeler, J. D. Rodick, C. M. Borduin, C. L. Hanson, S. M. Watson, and J. R. Urey, "Multisystemic treatment of juvenile offenders: Effects on adolescent behavior and family interaction," *Developmental Psychology, 22* (1986): 132–141; B. J. Mann, C. M. Borduin, S. W. Henggeler, and D. M. Blaske, "An investigation of systemic conceptualizations of parent-child coalitions and symptom change," *Journal of Consulting and Clinical Psychology, 58* (1990): 336–344; A. R. Nicol, J. Smith, B. Kay, D. Hall, J. Barlow, and B. Williams, "A focused casework approach to the treatment of child abuse: A controlled comparison," *Journal of Child Psychology and Psychiatry, 29* (1988): 703–711.

7. M. R. Dadds, M. R. Sanders, B. C. Behrens, and J. E. James, "Marital discord and child behavior problems: A description of family interactions during treatment," *Journal of Clinical Child Psychology, 16* (1987): 192–203.

8. E. M. Cummings and P. Davies, *Children and marital conflict: The impact of family dispute and resolution* (New York: Guilford Press, 1994).

9. K. S. Budd and T. P. O'Brien, "Father involvement in behavioral parent training: An area in need of research," *The Behavior Therapist, 5* (1982): 85–89; W. J. Doherty, "Involving the reluctant father in family therapy," in A. S. Gurman (ed.), *Questions and answers in the practice of family therapy* (Vol. 1) (New York: Brunner/Mazel, 1981), pp. 23–26; L. B. Feldman, "Fathers and fathering," in R. L. Meth and R. S. Pasick (eds.), *Men in therapy: The challenge of change* (New York: Guilford, 1990), pp. 88–107; T. Gaines, "Engaging the father in family therapy," in A. S. Gurman (ed.), *Questions and answers*

in the practice of family therapy (Vol. 1) (New York: Brunner/Mazel, 1981), pp. 20–22; L. Horton, "The father's role in behavioral parent training: A review," *Journal of Clinical Child Psychology, 13* (1984): 274–279; P. S. Penfold, "Parent's perceived responsibility for children's problems," *Canadian Journal of Psychiatry, 30* (1985): 255–258; E. M. Renouf, "Always on your mind but not always on your hands: Perspectives on parenting, particularly fatherhood," *Australian Journal of Marriage and Family, 12* (1991): 39–45; N. F. Russo, "Overview: Forging research priorities for women's mental health," *American Psychologist, 45* (1990): 368–373; B. Sachs, "Mastering the resistance of working-class fathers to family therapy," *Family Therapy, 13* (1986): 121–132.

10. W. J. Doherty, "Involving the reluctant father in family therapy," in A. S. Gurman (ed.), *Questions and answers in the practice of family therapy* (Vol. 1) (New York: Brunner/Mazel, 1981), pp. 23–26; F. Guillebeaux, C. L. Storm, and A. Demaris, "Luring the reluctant male: A study of males participating in marriage and family therapy," *Family Therapy, 13* (1986): 215–225; A. Lazar, A. Sagi, and M. W. Fraser, "Involving fathers in social services," *Children and Youth Services Review, 13* (1991): 287–300.

11. A. Lazar et al., "Involving fathers in social services," *Children and Youth Services Review, 13* (1991): 287–300.

12. L. L. Hecker, "Where is Dad?: 21 ways to involve fathers in family therapy," *Journal of Family Psychotherapy, 2* (1991): 31–45.

13. J. M. Bailey, D. Bobrow, M. Wolfe, and S. Mikach, "Sexual orientation of adult sons of gay fathers," *Developmental Psychology, 31* (1995): 124–129; J. J. Bigner and R. B. Jacobsen, "Adult responses to child behavior and attitudes toward fathering: Gay and nongay fathers," *Journal of Homosexuality, 23* (1992): 99–112; F. W. Bozett (ed.), *Gay and lesbian parents* (New York: Praeger, 1987); G. L. Greif and J. Kristall, "Common themes in a group for noncustodial parents," *Families in Society, 74* (1993): 240–245; J. W. Jacobs, "The effect of divorce on fathers: An overview of the literature," *American Journal of Psychiatry, 139* (1982): 1235–1241; J. W. Jacobs, "Treatment of divorcing fathers: Social and psychotherapeutic considerations," *American Journal of Psychiatry, 140* (1983): 1294–1299; M. S. Kiselica, J. Stroud, J. Stroud, and A. Rotzien, "Counseling the forgotten client: The teen father," *Journal of Mental Health Counseling, 14* (1992): 338–350; M. McGoldrick, J. Giordano, and J. K. Pearce, *Ethnicity and family therapy* (2nd ed.) (New York: Guilford, 1996); C. J. Tillitski,

"Fathers and child custody: Issues, trends, and implications for counseling," *Journal of Mental Health Counseling, 14* (1992): 351–361.

14. Consumer Reports, "Mental health: Does therapy work?" *Consumer Reports* (November 1995): 734–739.

15. G. O. Gabbard (ed.), *Sexual exploitation in professional relationships* (Washington, DC: American Psychiatric Press, 1989); H. S. Strean, *Therapists who have sex with their patients: Treatment and recovery* (New York: Brunner/Mazel, 1993).

CHAPTER 7

1. R. A. Barkley, *Defiant children: A clinician's manual for parent training* (New York: Guilford Press, 1987).

2. T. B. Brazelton, *Touchpoints: The essential reference* (Reading, MA: Addison-Wesley, 1992); J. P. Comer and A. F. Poussaint, *Raising black children* (New York: Penguin Books, 1992); S. deToledo and D. E. Brown, *Grandparents as parents: A survival guide for raising a second family* (New York: Guilford Press, 1995); D. Dinkmeyer and G. D. McKay, *Systematic training for effective parenting: The parent's handbook* (Circle Pines, MN: American Guidance Service, 1989); A. Farber and E. Mazlish, *How to talk so kids will listen and listen so kids will talk* (New York: Avon, 1980); L. Foust, *The single parent's almanac: Real world answers to everyday questions* (Rocklin, CA: Prima Publishing, 1996); S. H. Gookin, *Parenting for dummies* (Foster City, CA: IDG Books Worldwide, 1995); N. Kalter, *Growing up with divorce: Helping your child avoid immediate and later emotional problems* (New York: Free Press, 1990); T. McMahon, *Teen tips: A practical survival guide for parents with kids 11 to 19* (New York: Pocket Books, 1996); I. Ricci, *Mom's house, Dad's house: Making shared custody work* (New York: Macmillan, 1980); M. A. Straus and D. A. Donnelly, *Beating the devil out of them: Corporal punishment in American families* (New York: Lexington Books, 1994).

3. D. B. Jacobvitz and N. F. Bush, "Reconstructions of family relationships: Parent-child alliances, personal distress, and self-esteem," *Developmental Psychology, 32* (1996): 732–743; C. F. Johnson, "Detriangulation and conflict management in parent-adolescent relationships: A model," *Contemporary Family Therapy: An International Journal, 15* (1993): 185–195.

4. M. McGoldrick, *You can go home again: Reconnecting with your family* (New York: W. W. Norton, 1995); M. McGoldrick, J. Gior-

dano, and J. K. Pearce, *Ethnicity and family therapy* (2nd ed.) (New York: Guilford Press, 1996).

5. J. Cameron, *The artist's way* (New York: G. P. Putnam's Sons, 1992).

6. D. S. Becvar and R. J. Becvar, *Family therapy: A systemic integration* (2nd ed.) (Needham Heights, MA: Allyn and Bacon, 1993); J. L. Lebow and A. S. Gurman, "Research assessing couple and family therapy," *Annual Review of Psychology, 46* (1995): 27–57.

7. T. Arendell, *Fathers and divorce* (Thousand Oaks, CA: Sage 1995); E. Kruk, "The disengaged noncustodial father: Implications for social work practice with the divorced family," *Social Work, 39* (1994): 15–25.

8. W. Glennon, *Fathering: Strengthening connection with your children no matter where you are* (Berkeley, CA: Conari Press, 1995).

9. H. S. Sullivan and M. Klein, "The turning point: From psychobiology to object-relations," in H. Guntrip (ed.), *Psychoanalytic theory, therapy, and the self* (New York: Basic Books, 1973), pp. 45–68.

10. J. R. Fleck, C. C. Fuller, S. Z Malin, D. H. Miller, and K. R. Acheson, "Father psychological absence and heterosexual behavior, personal adjustment and sex-typing in adolescent girls," *Adolescence, 15* (1980): 847–860.

11. R. A. Barkley, *Defiant children: A clinician's manual for parent training* (New York: Guilford Press, 1987).

12. J. D. Eckler, *Step-by-stepparenting: A guide to successful living with a blended family* (Cincinnati, OH: Betterway Books, 1993); E. Einstein and L. Albert, *Strengthening your stepfamily* (Circle Pines, MN: American Guidance Service, 1986).

13. H. R. Clinton, *It takes a village and other lessons children teach us* (New York: Simon and Schuster, 1996); M. W. Edelman, *The measure of our success* (Washington, DC: Children's Defense Fund, 1993); J. A. Levine and E. W. Pitt, *New expectations: Community strategies for responsible fatherhood* (New York: Families and Work Institute, 1995); J. A. Levine, D. T. Murphy, and S. Wilson, *Getting men involved: Strategies for early childhood programs* (New York: Scholastic, 1993).

SELECTED BIBLIOGRAPHY

———————————•———————————

Arendell, Terry (1995). *Fathers and Divorce*. Thousand Oaks, CA: Sage.

Biller, Henry B. (1993). *Fathers and Families: Paternal Factors in Child Development*. Westport, CT: Auburn House.

Biller, Henry B., and Trotter, Robert J. (1994). *The Father Factor: What You Need to Know to Make a Difference*. New York: Pocket Books.

Caplan, Paula J. (1989). *Don't Blame Mother: Mending the Mother-Daughter Relationship*. New York: Harper and Row.

Coontz, Stephanie (1992). *The Way We Never Were: American Families and the Nostalgia Trap*. New York: Basic Books.

Cummings, E. Mark, and Davies, Patrick (1994). *Children and Marital Conflict: The Impact of Family Dispute and Resolution*. New York: Guilford Press.

Faludi, Susan (1991). *Backlash: The Undeclared War against American Women*. New York: Doubleday.

Griswold, Robert L. (1993). *Fatherhood in America: A History*. New York: Basic Books.

Hutchinson, E. O. (1992). *Black Fatherhood: The Guide to Male Parenting*. Los Angeles: Impact Publications.

Lamb, Michael E. (ed.) (1997). *The Role of the Father in Child Development* (3rd ed.). New York: Wiley.

Marsiglio, William (ed.) (1995). *Fatherhood: Contemporary Theory, Research, and Social Policy*. Thousand Oaks, CA: Sage.

Owen, Ursula (ed.) (1985). *Fathers: Reflections by Daughters*. New York: Pantheon Books.

Parke, Ross D. (1996). *Fatherhood*. Cambridge, MA: Harvard University Press.

Phares, Vicky (1996). *Fathers and Developmental Psychopathology*. New York: Wiley.

Powell, Joanna (ed.) (1994). *Things I Should Have Said to My Father: Poignant, Funny, and Unforgettable Remembrances from Memorable Sons*. New York: Avon Books.

Scull, Charles (ed.) (1992). *Fathers, Sons, and Daughters: Exploring Fatherhood, Renewing the Bond*. Los Angeles: Jeremy P. Tarcher.

Sullivan, Charles (1995). *Fathers and Children: In Literature and Art*. New York: Harry N. Abrams.

Willis, A. C. (1996). *Faith of Our Fathers: African-American Men Reflect on Fatherhood*. New York: Dutton.

INDEX

—————•—————

About the Author

VICKY PHARES is Associate Professor in the Department of Psychology at the University of South Florida in Tampa, Florida.